*What*

# THINK

*Becomes*

# YOUR REALITY

A Guide Towards Empowerment, Mindfulness and Fulfilment, using Disciplined Thinking

*Reginaldo Gattward*

What You Think Becomes Your Reality

Copyright © 2022 Reginaldo Gattward.

All rights reserved. Printed in the United Kingdom. No part of this book may be used or reproduced in any manner whatsoever without written permission except in the case of brief quotations em- bodied in critical articles or reviews.

This book is a work of fiction. Names, characters, businesses, organizations, places, events and incidents either are the product of the author's imagination or are used fictitiously. Any resemblance to actual persons, living or dead, events, or locales is entirely coincidental.

For information contact :

ReginaldoGattward@yahoo.com

Book and Cover designed by Reginaldo Gattward

ISBN: 9798824849875

First Edition: 2022

# Table of Contents

## INTRODUCTION ..........................................................1
### Grow Through Thinking ...................................................... 2
### Make Your Dreams Come True............................................ 7
### Why You Should Pursue Your Dreams ................................. 10
#### 1. It Will Make You Feel Good ..........................................10
#### 2. You Won't Have Any Regrets........................................10
#### 3. It fosters self-assurance. ............................................. 11
#### 4. Billionaires only have dreams. ......................................12
#### 5. Motivate Others...........................................................12

## CHAPTER ONE ....................................................... 14
### HAVING A DREAM AND FULFILLING IT........ 14
#### What Is Your Thought?.....................................................14
#### Before you take the test, make sure you know the answers..............14
#### The Right and Wrong Way to Imagine a Dream.............................15
#### 5 Reasons People Have Difficulty Identifying Their Dream ...............17
#### Are you prepared to put your ambition to the test?............................18
#### 20 GOALS AND DREAM OBJECTIVES (In no particular order): ....23
#### Why is it CRUCIAL To Pursue Your Dreams ?......................................24
#### Kicking Off in Seven Steps ...................................................27
##### Step 1: Visualize it. .........................................................27
##### Step 2: Have faith in it......................................................27
##### Step 3: Take a look at it....................................................28
##### Step 4: Tell it to someone. ...............................................28
##### Step 5: Make a plan. .......................................................29

- Step 7: Have fun with it. .................................................................. 30
  - 1. Develop a growth mentality. ........................................................ 30
  - 2. Develop faith in yourself. ............................................................. 31
  - 3. Develop a sense of impatience. ................................................... 32
  - 4. Foster Positive Interpersonal Relationships ............................... 33
  - 5. Thoughts Are Things, things may go wrong ............................. 34
- Be a Child again, Dream Big ............................................................... 36
  - #1 You are what you think. ............................................................. 36
  - #2 Your concentration is shifting, Focus. ...................................... 38
  - #3 Suddenly, your life takes a turn for the better. ........................ 40
  - #4 — Self-improvement as a requirement rather than a choice. ...... 41
  - #5 You can recover faster if you fail. ............................................. 42
  - #6 Manage your time more successfully. ...................................... 43
  - #7 The term "impossible" no longer applies to you. ..................... 44
  - #8 You start looking for motivation from people who have achieved. ............................................................................................ 45
  - #9 — When negative habits stifle your progress, become more aware ! ................................................................................................ 46
  - #10 You begin to obsess over minor details. ................................. 47
  - #11 Your tiny accomplishments add up over time ....................... 48

# CHAPTER TWO ................................................................................. 50

# SELF-ESTEEM ..................................................................................... 50

- Building Your Self-esteem ..................................................................... 50
  - 1. Take Small Steps to Get There ..................................................... 50
  - 2. Recognize Your Weaknesses and Strengths ............................... 50
  - 3. Fake It Until It is Real .................................................................... 51
  - 4. Acknowledge and Accept Criticism ............................................ 51

- 5. Treat yourself as though you were your best friend. ...... 51
- 6. When making decisions, trust your instincts. ............... 52
- 7. Do things for yourself, not for others. .......................... 52
- 8. Someone will always be better than you. ..................... 53

Improving Your Self-Esteem ................................................ 53
- Invest in your relationships. ............................................ 53
- Everything you do should be done with love. ................ 54
- Make big goals for yourself (in 10X) ............................... 55
- Be Prepared to Fail ........................................................... 55
- Your Life Should Be Shaped by Gratitude ...................... 56

Empowerment builds Self-Esteem ...................................... 57
- 1. Do it properly. .............................................................. 57
- 2. Give your all. ................................................................ 58
- 3. Treat others as you would want to be treated. ........... 59

From Self-esteem to Self-Confidence ................................. 62
- 1. Everything will work out just fine. .............................. 62
- 2. Speak the truth ............................................................. 62
- 3. Your words and actions have value. ............................ 63
- 4. We are all inconsequential in the grand scheme of things. ........... 63
- 5. Do not be frightened. ................................................... 64

Boosting your self-esteem .................................................... 65

# CHAPTER THREE .......................................................... 68

# FOCUS ON YOURSELF ................................................. 68

For a Successful and Fulfilling Life ..................................... 68
- 1. Have faith in yourself yet recognize your limitations. ........... 68
- 2. Simplify and de-clutter ................................................. 69
- 3. Everything should be used in moderation. ................. 70

4. Maintain a sense of perspective ...................................................... 70

5. Be attentive to the need of others. .................................................. 71

6. Prioritize your family. ..................................................................... 71

7. Pay attention to what is going on right now. ................................. 72

8. Maintain a positive outlook ............................................................ 72

9. Continue your education. ............................................................... 73

10. Have a strong desire for something. ............................................. 73

11. Be contemplative at all times ........................................................ 74

12. Surround yourself with encouraging individuals. ....................... 75

13. Remove the word "perfection" from your vocabulary. ............... 75

14. Either fix it or cope with it, but do not complain about it. ......... 75

15. Make a list of things for which you are grateful. ........................ 76

16. It is possible to have it all, but not all at the same time. ............ 77

How Do They Become Successful ? ..................................................... 78

Rules That Will Help YOU Succeed ................................................... 81

What You Think Becomes Your Reality #2 ........................................ 86

YOU, Creating Your Future Reality Through Thinking .................... 88

#1 — Have a clear understanding of what you want and why you want it. ............................................................................................... 90

#2 — Make and stick to a large-scale action plan. .......................... 92

#3 — Keep track of and analyse your outcomes, making adjustments as needed. ................................................................... 93

Yourself in a Better Position for Success ............................................ 95

From Those Who Know What They are Doing ............................... 101

# CHAPTER FOUR ............................................................................ 106

# BUSINESS MIND ............................................................................ 106

Personal Rules .................................................................................... 106

Defying all odds to find greatness. ...................................................... 108

Great Entrepreneurs' Business Rules ................................................ 113

   1. Believe in and commit to your business. .................................... 115

   2. Distribute Profits to Your Partners (Employees) ........................ 115

   3. Inspire your teammates, challenge them, and keep track of their progress ................................................................................................ 115

   4. Make sure you communicate everything. ................................... 116

   5. Keep an eye on your spending. .................................................... 116

   6. Begin small and work your way up .............................................. 116

   7. Concentrate on your primary business. ....................................... 117

   8. Make sure you have a compelling business concept. ................. 117

   9. Make sure you are pursuing your goals with a clear vision. ...... 118

   10. Build your company one step at a time. .................................... 118

   11. Do not force the creation of a new market. ............................... 118

   12. MAKE YOURSELF READY FOR THE WORST ................... 119

   13. ALWAYS READ BEFORE GOING ABOUT YOUR DAY-TO-DAY ACTIVITIES ............................................................................... 119

   14. Be Honest to Yourself ................................................................. 120

   15. Do Not Let Your Business Ownership Pass You By Your Reality Will Be Clouded By Your Dreams. ..................................................... 120

   16. Great products and services at a fair price. ............................... 121

# CHAPTER FIVE ........................................................ 122

## BECOME DISCIPLINED... ................................... 122

...ON ACHIEVING YOUR GOALS ................................................. 122

Set goals that motivate you. ............................................................... 122

Take the initiative ................................................................................ 123

There will be no more negative. ......................................................... 123

Maintain a healthy balance ................................................................. 124

Take it apart ........................................................................................ 124

Be willing to fail .................................................................................. 125

Inform everyone .................................................................................. 125

Keep tabs on your development .......................................................... 126

Create a mental image of the final product ........................................ 126

Motivational Rules to Help You Achieve Your Life Goals ................ 127

...ON ACHIEVING YOUR OBJECTIVES ....................................... 136

    1. Set SMARTER objectives. ........................................................ 139

    2. Make a strategy for moving forward. ......................................... 139

    3. Get rid of undesirable behaviours. .............................................. 140

    4. Instil self-control. ........................................................................ 141

    5. Keep your distractions to a minimum. ....................................... 141

    6. Use everyday goal-setting to your advantage. ............................ 142

    7. Stay away from procrastination. ................................................. 143

    8. Keep track of your time. ............................................................. 144

    9. Make a bee-line towards the frog. .............................................. 146

    10. Put the Pareto Principle in action. ........................................... 146

    11. Failure is a good thing. ............................................................. 147

    12. Find ways to be inspired every day. ......................................... 147

    13. Look for a role model. .............................................................. 148

    14. Maintain a record of your achievements. ................................. 149

    15. Be open to feedback. ................................................................ 149

    16. Maintain a tidy working environment. .................................... 150

    17. Get out of bed as soon as possible. ........................................... 150

    18. Make the most of your free time on the weekends. ................. 151

    19. Enlist the assistance of others. .................................................. 151

20. Take on the job. .................................................................... 152

21. Check in on your progress regularly. ......................................... 153

22. Use incentives to keep oneself motivated. ................................ 153

**CONCLUSION** ............................................................ 154

# **INTRODUCTION**

When they realize they will never be flawless because too many people decide to give up. "What is the point?" they ask themselves. Life is a journey, not a destination. We have this life to learn, grow, and become the best versions of ourselves. What is the point? We carry what we learn in this life in the following. Whatever information and intellect, we get through hard work will provide us with a significant advantage in the future. It is not about being better than anyone else. It is about becoming the best version of yourself. Our goal should be to become better today than yesterday and better tomorrow than today. It is a continuous and never-ending improvement.

## Grow Through Thinking

Everything is in a state of vibration, according to both of them. This is undeniably true. This has been confirmed by science. Everything, including the matter, vibrates. You share the same state when you can turn anything into the same vibration as something else. A good illustration of this is radios. When a transmission station is set on a specific vibration or frequency, a reception station (like your car radio) can and will take what is delivered.

The mind is both a sender and a receiver of vibrations. This is a common occurrence. You can sense other people's vibes. When someone is in a good mood or a poor mood, you can sense. We have all encountered people who seem to radiate those energies. You'll notice it soon enough.

You must be in a positive vibe yourself to receive positive vibrations. It is a straightforward concept. The challenging aspect is to maintain that good attitude and mindset. This is especially difficult if negative individuals and situations surround you.

Keep your objectives and ambitions in your mind and forethought while maintaining this optimistic mindset and energy. You will manifest in your life whatever you think about. If you desire anything (such as a goal or a car), keep it in mind. You will find ways to obtain it.

Whatever you think becomes you. Earl Nightingale constantly highlighted this. You are going to be successful if you think about it. Likewise, you will fail if you concern yourself with failure. So, you cannot be anything if you do not think about it. That is all there is to talk about. If you want to be an astronaut and study criminology, you have little or no chance of becoming an astronaut.

That is the most basic definition of a dream. If a dream does not turn into a vision, it may fail along the way.

So, if you can visualize it, you can achieve it.

This is only true if you also think you can accomplish the task.

So, hoping is not enough; believing in what you want or hope for is essential to see it come true.

"If wishes were horses, even beggars would ride," someone once said.

Many people have dreams, but there are very few who feel they can attain them.

Make sure you're not falling into the trap of pursuing a dream you do not believe in. Do not be compelled to do something you disagree with.

You may have many dreams, but you also talk about believing in them. Once you have a desire that excites you and strengthens your belief in your ability to attain it, it is only a matter of time before it becomes a reality.

The essence of this saying is that you would not have created the dream if you could not realize it, which should give you confidence that you can.

**You must take your vision to the land where it will become a reality.**

A dream is a wish by definition. However, a vision is a more explicit version of that dream. The goal has been defined, and the next step is figuring out how to get there.

So, do not follow in the footsteps of others because you see them succeed. It could be the most perilous step you have ever taken.

Do not let yourself get caught in a dream you do not think you can achieve. Instead, focus on what you truly believe in.

## If you can think of it, you can achieve it.

Here are some pointers on how to go about reaching your dreams.

1. Articulate your 'dream' - Articulating your dreams is the first and most crucial step in realizing them. In this case, a 'dream' is a professional aspiration. For example, a bigger car may be something you want, but it is not a professional goal. A 'dream' would be to succeed in your start-up and eventually export your items to other countries. A 'dream' could also be to become a successful artist by having your work recognized by the art world and exhibited in a foreign nation. This type of professional desire can assist the dreamer to develop a sense of long-term motivation and continue forward on the route to success.

2. Be willing to put in much effort - Realizing a vision can take a long time. When asked about his "genius," legendary inventor Thomas Edison said, "Genius is an inspiration to one per cent and perspiration to ninety-nine per cent. You know, inspiration comes from a dream. The amount of sweat you put in, or the amount of work you put in, will influence whether or not your idea becomes a reality. An excellent idea is only the start; it is not a guarantee of success.

3. Keep a positive attitude when faced with failure. Taking failure in stride can help you traverse the ups and downs of day-to-day living, which are unavoidable in any worthwhile endeavour. There will be some dark periods on the road. It will help if you do not allow them to deter you from continuing on your route. If you have unrealistic expectations regarding the reward you think you deserve for your efforts today, you will undoubtedly lose your motivation. Make an effort to have a positive attitude and learn from your failures. The ability to avoid making the same mistake is the mark of a great leader.

4. Take pleasure in your achievements. If you keep putting up the necessary work, success will come to you. Take the time to appreciate them. Savouring success can assist in re-energize the spirit and creating motivation for future attempts. Taking pleasure in your accomplishments will help make the road worthwhile. Both the route and the destination are equally significant. Time is a limited resource that may never be replenished.

5. Have a support structure. Very few of the most significant achievements in history were achieved by people who worked alone. On the road to success, having a solid support system is essential. Identify and keep in touch with a core group of individuals who support you. Making sacrifices to pursue a desire will require you to communicate with your loved ones

and help them understand your priorities. If they understand, they will be more willing to support you. Beyond emotional support, having a source of expertise and assistance may make a tremendous difference, especially in the early stages of beginning a firm.

## Make Your Dreams Come True

1. Decide what you want to achieve. Some of us have so many dreams spinning through our heads that we do not know where to start. In comparison, others cannot seem to pick just one. Whether publishing a book, running a marathon, buying a house, or finding true love, the path to fulfilment always begins with the deliberate identification of a single goal and the deep resolve to achieve it. Allow yourself some time. Choose one, then get to work on achieving it.

2. Have faith in your ability to achieve it. Too many people, unfortunately, will never achieve their goals because they fail to believe in themselves. Optimism is essential for achieving one's goals and enjoying one's life. If you do not believe in yourself, making it your main objective should be your priority. If you do have self-confidence, start channelling it toward your desired outcome.

3. Seek assistance. There have been others who have gone before you. Take in as much information as you can from them. Don't let your pride be the only thing standing between you and them. Instead, be modest and beg for assistance.

4. Make any required adjustments to your life. By definition, if you have not achieved your goal yet, you will need to change your way of life to do so. While some of the changes may be significant, they always begin small:

• Running a marathon begins with a one-mile run.
• Deciding on a topic is the first step in writing a book.
• Begin decluttering your home by cleaning one drawer, closet, or room.
• Changing one meal can help you lose 50 pounds.
• Saving one pound is the first step toward purchasing a home.

To achieve your goals, you will need to modify your way of life. It is one tiny step at a time. Moreover, while there are many steps to take, the good news is that the first one is quite doable. The second is the same.

5. Establish a deadline. Deadlines compel us to act and force us to make decisions. As a result, it is critical to set a realistic timeframe and get started. Purchase a home within the following three years. In the coming year, work on your

marriage. In the following six months, lose 20 pounds. Alternatively, start a blog within the following 30 days. Find a day, a calendar, and a red marker. Make a circle around it. After all, a wish is nothing more than a fantasy without a deadline.

6. Inform others because sharing your dreams with others provided you with an endless supply of inspiration. The number of people who are rooting for me increases by a factor of two. It soon triples.

7. Maintain your concentration. Dreams, by their very nature, necessitate patience. Along the journey, there will be victories and setbacks. Those who continue despite setbacks will realize their ambitions. Those that give up will be sent back to the first step. Furthermore, why would you want to start over if you have already come this far? Instead of allowing setbacks to derail your ambitions, utilize them to refocus your efforts and resolve.

# Why You Should Pursue Your Dreams

## 1. It Will Make You Feel Good

What makes you truly happy is something you understand on a deep level. This joy can pervade all aspects of our life.

This delight is intertwined with our dreams. Keep in mind that your heart is constantly looking out for your best interests. It is in your best interest to be happy. You're never going to be sad one day in your life if you are happy to do what you do every day.

## 2. You Won't Have Any Regrets

Even in a house full of people, we have to live with ourselves. Your heart, or that small voice inside you (which we affectionately refer to as the inner voice), is constantly conversing with us. It could be a nagging voice of reality or an inner advisor to help you achieve your objectives.

**Why Should You Pursue Your Dreams?**

Indeed, not doing what we want in life is going to lead to regret. The reason for this is that our desires, our goals, are sometimes so great that they leave us with little room to do anything else.

By listening to that inner voice, you will never have to regret not being able to achieve your goals.

## 3. It fosters self-assurance.

Trying to ignore your dreams is difficult when you think about it. You must essentially ignore yourself 24 hours a day, seven days a week. On the other hand, following your dreams may appear to be a daunting task, yet the steps are there if you listen and pay attention.

You're developing a feeling of self-trust that most people never achieve by listening to your inner voice and following your aspirations. This self-confidence is essential for leading a life of clarity and a deeper understanding of oneself than most.

It is not as challenging as it appears. Just keep in mind that everything should be done one step at a time. You will get there in the end.

## 4. Billionaires only have dreams.

This is correct. How many people have gotten wealthy and successful by doing something they did not give their all?

Your dreams, you know, are a blueprint for what you will do with your life. This is essentially a combination of your calling, purpose, and destiny.

It does not work if you are working on something you enjoy. Suddenly, you are constructing the path to your ideal one step at a time. Life is a playground. It should be used to its full potential. Invest in what makes you happy.

## 5. Motivate Others

We live in a world where many people feel unable to do what they truly want, which is both an opportunity and a tragedy. However, if you act and decide that you want to live the life you have always imagined, you will be able to do this.

Of course, this may appear to be a positive spin to start the engine going, but it is not. We were created for excellence as people. As creators, we have a responsibility to improve the world we live in. In many ways, our dreams change the world.

You're not only satisfying your inner fire, but you are also encouraging others to do the same. Nothing is more essential than just following the heart and becoming an example of greatness.

Everything in life takes time, which necessitates a certain amount of patience. The most challenging aspect of this entire procedure is the practice of patience. However, this comes with increased awareness of what it takes to achieve your goals and the resulting peace.

# CHAPTER ONE

## HAVING A DREAM AND FULFILLING IT

### What Is Your Thought?

The majority of people have no notion of how to realize their ambitions. They only have a hazy idea of what they would like to do or someone they would like to be eventually. However, they have no idea how to go from here to there. If that fits you, you will be relieved to learn that there is still hope.

### Before you take the test, make sure you know the answers.

Do you recall a teacher giving a review before an exam and stating something along the lines of, "Pay attention now, since this will be on the test?" Teachers who genuinely want to see their students succeed frequently state things like this. They desired that we be well-prepared so that we might perform successfully. They put us to the test, but they also put us in a position to succeed.

My ambition is to be one of those motivating instructors for you. I want to help you prepare to put your dream to the test so that you can make it a reality. How? If you know the correct questions to ask yourself and can answer them positively, you will have a good chance of achieving your goals. The more questions you can answer affirmatively, the more likely you are to succeed!

## The Right and Wrong Way to Imagine a Dream

- Daydreams—distractions from current work
- Pie-in-the-Sky Dreams—Irrational ideas with no strategy or foundation in reality
- Bad Dreams—fear and paralysis-inducing worries
- Idealistic Dreams—how the world would be if you were in charge
- Vicarious Dreams—dreams lived through others
- Romantic Dreams—belief that someone will make you happy
- Destination Dreams—belief that a place or lifestyle will make you happy
- Career Dreams—belief that a position, title, or award will make you happy

Material Dreams—the assumption that having much money or having much stuff will make you happy.

## What are decent dreams, true dreams worthy of a person's existence, except these?

A dream is an energizing vision of the future that energizes your mind, will, emotions and motivates you to do everything in your power to make it a reality. An image and plan of an individual's goal and potential is an objective that deserves to be pursued. "A dream is the seed of possibility sown in the soul of a human being, calling him to take a unique route to the realization of his destiny," says one of my friends.

## So, what exactly do you have in mind?

Dreams are rare and valuable. They help us move forward. They provide us with vitality. They elicit our enthusiasm. Everyone should have a fantasy.
Nevertheless, what if you are not sure whether you want to pursue a dream? Let us be honest. Many people are discouraged from pursuing their dreams. Others have ambitions but have given up hope and put them away.

You can locate or reclaim your dreams. Furthermore, they do not have to be large ambitions; not all dreams are worth pursuing. They must be more significant than you. "Dreams arrive in sizes that are too huge for us to fit into."

If you've given up hope, lost sight of your dream, or never connected with something worth dreaming about and striving toward. Perhaps learning about the five most prevalent reasons why people struggle to define their dream would be beneficial:

## 5 Reasons People Have Difficulty Identifying Their Dream

1. Others have discouraged some people from dreaming. Many people have had their aspirations snatched from under their feet! Dream killers and idea killers abound in the world.

2. Past disappointments and sorrows might stymie some people. Disappointment is the difference between what one expects and what one gets. All of us have crossed that chasm. "I will never do that again!" we exclaim when something goes awry. What a blunder, especially in terms of our dreams! We must pay the price of failure to achieve success.

3. Some people fall into the trap of settling for mediocrity. "The minute you accept for less than you deserve, you get even less," writes Maureen Dowd, a columnist. Dreams necessitate a person's willingness to expand, to go above and

beyond the norm. You cannot pursue your dreams while remaining comfortably average. The two are mutually exclusive.

4. Some people lack the self-assurance required to follow their ambitions. "It takes much courage to tell someone else about your dreams." It takes courage to talk about a dream, and even more, courage to follow through on it. Moreover, sometimes, confidence distinguishes individuals who dream and follow their goals from those who do not.

5. Some people cannot dream due to a lack of imagination. How do people find out what they want to accomplish with their lives? By imagining! That may seem unduly basic, but it is the starting point. Imagination is the fertile ground on which a dream might grow.

## Are you prepared to put your ambition to the test?

You might be thinking to yourself, "Okay, I have had a dream." I believe it is worthwhile to pursue. So, what is next? How do I know I have a good chance of succeeding?

This leads to the following questions:
- The Ownership Issue: Is my dream truly mine?
- The Clarity Question: Can I see my dream?

- The Reality Check: Will I be able to realize my dream if I rely on elements within my control?
- The Passion Question: Do I feel compelled to pursue my dream?
- The Pathway Question: Do I have a plan in place to help me achieve my goals?
- The People Question: Have I thought about whom I'll need to make my goal a reality?
- The Cost Question: Will I Be Willing to Pay for My Dream?
- The Tenacity Test: Am I Getting Any Closer to My Goal?
- The Fulfilment Question: Does pursuing my dream bring me happiness?
- The Importance Question: Will my dream helps others?

"Remember that in this world, there are only two types of people: realists and dreamers." The realists are well aware of their destination. The visionaries have already arrived. You are ready to put your dream to the test and begin to realize it now that you have recognized it.

**Is it possible for you to say yes to the question, "What is my dream?"**

If you are not sure what your dream is either because you are afraid to dream or because you've lost track of it, then start preparing yourself to accept it by looking into the following:

- Mental preparation: Read and study the topics that interest you the most.
- Experiential preparation: Participate in activities linked to your areas of interest.
- Visual preparation: Hang photographs of people and objects that inspire you.
- Prepare to be a hero by reading about and meeting individuals you admire and who inspire you.
- Physical Preparation: Get in the best shape of your life to pursue your passion.
- Spiritual preparation: Seek God's guidance in realizing a larger-than-life ambition.

Focus on uncovering your goal once you have completed these six steps to place yourself in the greatest possible position to receive one. Keep in mind, "A dream is what you want if everything and <u>everything</u> is feasible."

So, what are our options? How can we get from not knowing what we want to know what we want? How do we transition from self-doubt to a genuine feeling of meaning and purpose? How can we become our source of inspiration and generate happiness from inside, rather than relying on anything external to make us happy and enthusiastic, such as our relationship, money, or the weather?

One of the most effective methods is to tap into our deepest wants, envision beautiful fantasies, and make exciting goals that fulfil those aspirations. Then, of course, we must take steps to make our ambitions and desires a reality.

However, let us not merely make goals because we believe we should. Instead, ponder what is about to transform your life completely. What is going to make you feel truly incredible? Let us start with the FEELING and work our way up to the DREAMING.

No problem if you consider yourself a realistic person who believes being a dreamer is too fairy-tale. We can redo it. Instead of daydreaming, let us construct a list of goals that you'd like to achieve and that will make you feel great.

You are not sure what makes you feel great? Oh no. It appears that we have some work ahead of us. Don't worry, my Zen-warrior-in-training, have some faith. The inspiration, energy, and passion are all present and accounted for. We may gradually entice it out again. Just do not give up on your ideas and objectives before you have even started. Allow yourself to dream again as if you were a child.

Do you dislike the idea of establishing goals? I recommend that you follow Snoop Dogg's lead and ditch this restrictive mental habit like it's hot. There is nothing wrong with having desires for yourself and others. That is fantastic if you consider yourself a free spirit. Yes, I agree! Is there, however, any danger in deciding on a course for your life? Certainly not. We can have a free spirit while also setting goals. The two are not mutually exclusive. There is nothing cold, corporate, or materialistic about it, and setting goals will not make you a jerk (and going after them like a bull at a gate).

Declaring yourself, "I am not the type of person who sets objectives," is like locking your heart in a cage and condemning yourself to a life of mediocrity. Setting objectives and wishing for beautiful things in life provides fuel for joy and happiness. Let us get rid of the stigma and do it anyway. Do you have any idea what you're looking for? See the two paragraphs above and below for more information.

Are you afraid to set a goal because you are afraid you will not get there? It is not going to make your heart sing to spend your entire life on the couch. It is time to get ready to fail at anything. This is so crucial that I am going to CAP it. So it is crystal clear. IF YOU DO NOT MEET YOUR GOAL, IT IS NOT A BIG DEAL, EVER! All that matters is that you have a strong desire for something.

It is the desire, dreaming, striving, and pursuing something that makes life worthwhile. THE JOURNEY is another name for it.

Here are 20 goals from people I know, if you think your desires are too foolish, senseless, unreachable, or any other judgment you might place on yourself. Some of these are guiding principles to follow. Some of them are corny, while others are absurd. It does not matter. You may do whatever you want. Furthermore, do not even try to excuse it.

## 20 GOALS AND DREAM OBJECTIVES (In no particular order):

1. To constantly live and love courageously.
2. Publish a best-selling book about enlightened life.
3. Do yoga every day for the next 20 years.
4. Become a Monk.
5. Get a surfboard and surf barrels all over the world.
6. Play a leading role in a Hollywood action film.
7. Get to know my soon-to-be hubby. Allow me to be deeply in love with him and to be deeply loved in return. Marry that man who is a legend.
8. Travel across the world by bicycle.
9. Host a massive bash in the South of France. Fly over and bring as many pals as you can.
10. Learn how to ride a Warrior Horse in Mongolia.
11. Participate in the Olympic Games.
12. Have a large, inviting, lovely home by the sea with a magnificent flower and vegetable garden.

13. Become a boxing champion.
14. Begin a revolution and inspire others to do the same.
15. Spend three months in Paris.
16. Return to the Solomon Islands to work on the development of women's leadership.
17. Contribute to the reduction of poverty around the world.
18. Become a world renowned tycoon.
19. Go whale shark swimming.
20. Every day, provide love, peace, and joy to the globe.

Okay, that is enough for me. How about you?
What is one single desire or goal that you want to achieve in your life?

## Why is it CRUCIAL To Pursue Your Dreams ?

1. The secret of living is giving. If you follow your dreams, you will have something worth sharing with others, such as hope, inspiration, and a reason to live. In my opinion, it is a significant contribution.

2. Pursuing your dreams will increase your bravery. Courage is the fuel that allows you to accomplish incredible achievements in life, follow your dreams, and be courageous. You will undoubtedly become unstoppable in due time.

3. There is a reason we liked magic and dreams as children. Stop chasing your dreams, and you will forget what it is like to be young and eager.

4. Great dreamers learn to be self-sufficient, realizing that they can make a difference independently.

5. Dreams might help you forget about the bad things that happen in life. You will decide if your dreams or the drama is more essential. When you are passionate about pursuing your dreams, drama tends to fade away.

6. It provides you with something to share with and inspire your children. You have demonstrated that everything is possible if you set your mind to it.

7. By reaching your goals, you will learn to enjoy the experience of failure and understand that failure is a necessary part of success. It was not all that horrible in the end.

8. Regret is a dreadful thing. A dream can bring you to regret if you do not at least try to follow it.

9. You can never be too old to dream. When we know what we desire, age is irrelevant.

10. You become a fascinating person who demonstrates to others that you have a sense of meaning, direction, and purpose.

11. The unknown of pursuing your aspirations may generate some anxiety. However, it is okay because fear is supposed to make you feel more alive.

12. It is much fun to prove the world incorrect. So why would you want to stick with the status quo?

13. As we discover that anything is possible, the lines of the boundaries that the world places in front of us begin to vanish as we pursue and achieve our aspirations.

14. You are the first to witness your desire come true when you achieve it. You can brag about your achievements to the rest of the world. Nevertheless, you were in the front row on a single chair to witness the miracle.

15. Your dreams have no boundaries. You are the one that creates them, big and small. When you understand this, you may devise a strategy to help you plan and achieve your end goal.

16. A dream may define you. Once realised, you can show others that they have no control over what you can or cannot be.

# Kicking Off in Seven Steps

## Step 1: Visualize it.

It all begins in mind and heart. Every great accomplishment originated in one person's thinking. They dared to dream, to believe it could be done. Allow yourself to wonder, "What if?" for a while. Consider the big picture. Do not let negative thoughts get the best of you. You want to be a "dreamer," don't you? Consider the opportunities that await you, your family, and others. Re-ignite your dreams if you have let them go cold. Keep the fires burning. It is far too short to waste it.

## Step 2: Have faith in it.

Yes, you must have a big dream. It should be something that appears to be beyond your ability. However, it must be credible. You need to be able to claim that if some things happen, other things help. If you work hard enough, you can achieve your goal, even a lofty one. Someone without a college education might dream of building a £50-million worth company in a year. That is a huge claim, but it is plausible.

A bad example would be expecting a 90-year-old woman with arthritis to run a marathon in under three hours. It is significant, but it is also impossible. Instead, she should concentrate on growing a £50 million worth company in a year! Moreover, she had better start moving!

## Step 3: Take a look at it.

Great achievers have a pattern. They can "see" things. Even when sitting in a folding chair in their garage "headquarters," they imagine themselves roaming around their CEO office in their new £25 million corporate headquarters. In the NBA, great free-throw shooters visualize the ball going through the basket. The ball should travel straight down the fairway, according to PGA golfers. Speakers who aspire to be world-class believe they speak with passion and emotion. All of this prepares the mind to direct the body's actions to carry out the dream.

## Step 4: Tell it to someone.

Many dreams never come true because the dreamer keeps everything to himself. It is a peaceful dream that only exists in his head. Those who desire to realize their dreams must convey their stories to a large number of people. One reason is that we are beginning to believe this. It has to be conceivable if we are talking about it. Another reason is that it makes us responsible. When we tell others, it motivates us to follow through. So we do not appear silly.

## Step 5: Make a plan.

Every dream necessitates the creation of a strategy. The ancient adage "you get what you plan for" holds in this case. It is not going to happen on its own. You must sit down regularly to develop your approach to realizing your dream. Consider all of the particulars. Break the plan down into small, manageable chunks. Then give yourself a deadline for completing each action on your "dream plan."

## Step 6: Put it to use.

Wouldn't it be wonderful if we could go before this one? Unfortunately, the most successful people are also the most hardworking. While the rest of the world is watching TV on their sofas, achievers are working toward their goal of achieving their dream. I use the following formula: your short-term tasks multiplied by time equals your long-term achievements. If you work on it every day, you will eventually reach your goal. Page after page, War and Peace was written in longhand.

## Step 7: Have fun with it.

Be sure to have fun once you have reached your goal and live your dream. Take pleasure in the journey. Along the way, give yourself some incentives. When you get there, give yourself an enormous reward. Assist others in having fun. Be kind and giving in your actions. Make a difference in the lives of others by using your dream. Then return to step one. Moreover, this time, dream a little more fabulous!

## What You Think Becomes Your Reality #1

Use the following five strategies to help you achieve your goals:

## 1. Develop a growth mentality.

The fixed mindset and the developmental mindset are two types of mindsets that people might have.

The individual with a fixed mindset believes that leaders are born. This perspective prevents people from taking risks because they believe their fate has already been written for them.

A person with a growth mindset believes that you can attain your goals with practice, tenacity, and patience.

Only those who accept the growth mindset may benefit from it. Your brain can stretch once you accept a growth mentality. Moreover, like a rubber band, the brain extends in response to how much you use it.

With that perspective, you will build your strengths in the direction of your dreams since you will realize that dreams are accomplished not via birth but rather by putting forth maximum effort in pursuing them.

## 2. Develop faith in yourself.

Have faith in your abilities to achieve your goals. Get out of your comfort zone and try something new. Take chances and follow your passion every day.

Your dream is a reflection of who you are. You are the only one who can make it come true. You will stay in the same place if you do not take the risk of pursuing your ambition.

Prioritize your dream. Make a plan that will help you incorporate it into your everyday routine. You can keep your progress from being sabotaged by making it a daily habit.

Demonstrate to yourself that you are deserving of pursuing your dream. Stick with it for a long time, not just a few weeks or months. Make a concerted effort to realize your ambition.

The more confident you are in your ability to fulfil your dream, the more likely you are to achieve it. According to Richard Davidson of the University of Wisconsin, the expectation of accomplishing your goals motivates you to work harder toward them.

You will succeed if you believe in yourself.

## 3. Develop a sense of impatience.

Make pursuing your dream a daily priority. Commit never to defer working on your dream, even if you do not see immediate results or if the temptation to give up becomes overwhelming.

Allow the top performers in every sector to inspire you. They are consistent and show up. Deliver when everybody is bogged down by life and endless battle with procrastination.

Please think of the kids who waited fifteen minutes to eat their marshmallows because they wanted an extra one. According to a follow-up study, the children who wait to develop more extraordinary social skills are more successful.

Choose discipline over pain and work on your dream every day, no matter how difficult things become. Even if you do not see the results right away, the satisfaction you will experience when your hard work is rewarded will be worth waiting for.

## 4. Foster Positive Interpersonal Relationships

Humans are designed to interact with others. Relationships impact our mental health and give us a sense of purpose and significance in life. Make healthy connections a significant priority in your life if you want to achieve your goals because you will need other people to succeed.

As a result, surround yourself with joyful individuals who will make you happy. Avoid toxic people that constantly sabotage your goals. Their pessimism will eventually cause you to question your dreams. Seek out people who will encourage you to believe in yourself and your objectives.

Gratitude is a good thing to cultivate.

Your willpower is strengthened by gratitude. It keeps you focused on functioning well, allowing you to act with confidence rather than allowing your anxieties to get in the way.

Everyone can be thankful. You have something to be grateful for whether you are sick or well, young or old, as long as you ate today and your heart is pumping.

The most successful people in life are those who are always appreciative. Regardless of their circumstances, they see the world as a place brimming with possibilities.

Regardless of your circumstances, choose gratitude. Furthermore, consider it a blessing that you have the chance to pursue your dream.

Demonstrate to yourself that you are capable of accomplishing your goals.

Staying focused on your dream will help you achieve this.

Continue cultivating a growth attitude, faith in your dream, delayed gratification, good relationships, and gratitude slowly and steadily.

Because there is no such thing as natural talent, it all comes down to effort and perseverance.

Besides, if you do, you will personally see what it is like to achieve your ambition.

## 5. Thoughts Are Things, things may go wrong

Success and wealth are what dreams entail holding on to the picture of a better life. Although it can be challenging to achieve, it is undoubtedly helpful with setbacks and disappointments along the way. Anyone who has accomplished a significant objective can attest to the validity of this statement.

Even though some of us enjoy dreaming, we each dream in our unique way. We do not always cling to our dreams, even if we know that we can and will do whatever is necessary to make them a reality.

The truth is, many of us abandon our ambitions.

When things go wrong, we give up, as they say. Instead of going through the agony and pain of another failure, we give up.

However, being a starry-eyed dreamer does not imply giving up. Dreaming large and often actually provides us with a platform for success and progress.

Everything begins with a dream.

Although there are many benefits to living a "regular" life, complacency and compliance are carried out with calm behaviour. There is nothing like being a dreamer and having crazy ideas about life that you know you are meant to live, even if you are not living now.

## Be a Child again, Dream Big

Children have big dreams. It is a part of their genetic makeup or, to put it another way, their general makeup. They never think little because they are not bound by the same constraints that limit grownups. "I want two swimming pools!" a toddler could answer when asked what he wants for Christmas. One in the front and one in the backyard."

Although it is easy to dismiss a child's wishes as irrational or impossible, who can say it? Who is to say that any of our ambitions are ridiculous or unattainable? It is not impossible to do anything that goes against the grain or runs in the opposite direction of social conventions.

We could all benefit from a little childish merriment. There is nothing wrong with it at all. If your dreams do not terrify you, they are not large enough.
You are the only thing preventing you from reaching them. We may be our own greatest adversaries in many ways, especially when we do not trust in ourselves completely.

**#1 You are what you think.**

Dreamers are a local group of people. They have a unique ability to see things so vividly that they may virtually see them right before their eyes. Moreover, that carries a lot of weight and influence. Why? Because ideas are objects. We become what we think.

You've probably heard the phrase before, but here is why it is so effective. Anyone who has ever achieved extraordinary outcomes can visualize their goals before they become a reality vividly. This is something that every single person who has gone on to do something significant can attest to. Invariably, the dream comes as reality.

Why do you think the test drive is such a great selling feature when you go automobile shopping? Salespeople understand that once you get behind the wheel, the deal is almost done. One way to make a desire a reality is to physically drive a car and experience what it's like to drive. They are well aware of this.

Similarly, an open house or real estate tour is a handy tool. Because not everyone can visualize themselves living in a specific home, experiencing it first-hand can assist. Moreover, if the house is perfectly furnished to your taste, you are far more likely to envision yourself living there. As a result, you may be purchasing it.

**Everything is made of thoughts.**

Nothing could be more accurate. Dream big if you are a dreamer. See your dreams as plainly and vividly as the sun. Make a detailed list of them. Allowing others to discourage you because your goals are lofty is a mistake. They should be large enough to frighten you to death. It is at this point that you realize that you have something valid on your hands.

### #2 Your concentration is shifting, Focus.

Consider two people who attend the same event. An individual zeroes down on a couple squabbling in the corner, yelling at each other all the time. He describes the gathering as "terrible," claiming that all he saw was people arguing. Another person attends the same party, dances, laughs, makes new acquaintances, then comes home, telling everyone that this was one of the best nights of his life.

So, what is the difference between these two individuals?

Focus! It is all about focusing.

You get more of what you concentrate on. We will receive more of it if we concentrate on whatever we are talking about in life. Professional race car drivers are educated intensely about attention. Their eyes and heads should be looking when steering out of trouble because that is where your vehicle will end up.

You will strike the wall if you spin out of control and focus on it, scared, praying, and dreading you'll hit it. Why? You concentrated on it.

Similarly, those who have huge aspirations are laser-focused on achieving them. They eat, sleep, and live those fantasies. They have irrational imaginations about their dreams coming true. Furthermore, if they do not give up, those dreams will come true because they put their minds to them. Even when it seemed like they would crash and burn, they continued to navigate towards them.

Of course, nothing important comes easily. Nevertheless, the focus is one of the fundamental reasons why certain big dreamers can achieve incredible outcomes. Despite the sceptics and criticism that surrounds them, they persevere. However, their ambitious ambitions enable them to overcome their fears of failure and stumbling hurdles.

Do not be frightened to dream large. It will change your perspective. It will assist you in changing your mindset to propel you forward rather than hold you back. Ignore the sceptics. There will always be those who oppose you. Dream big, and do not be scared to follow your passions.

## #3 Suddenly, your life takes a turn for the better.

The subconscious mind has tremendous power. Even more so than modern science has revealed. In truth, we have just started to scratch the surface of what we know about the brain, mind and their roles in human consciousness. Nevertheless, without getting into a debate about the immensity of things beyond our comprehension, one thing is sure: the mind is powerful.

When you dream, you cling to ideas present in your conscious mind. Nevertheless, they also make their way into your subconscious mind. The subconscious mind assists in processing up to 60,000 thoughts per day, which is a staggering figure when you consider it. Those ideas are in charge of every moment and movement you make in life.

What you think influences what you feel. What you feel influences how you behave, which influences your life experiences and your values and beliefs. Therefore, these thoughts (many of which come from the subconscious mind) have a meaningful influence on your life.

You must control your ideas if you want to control the direction in which you are going. When you dream big, you think about abundance rather than scarcity. Even if you are in a condition of severe need, broken, or have repeatedly failed, as long as you can dream large. The trajectory of your life and its outcome will shift.

## #4 — Self-improvement as a requirement rather than a choice.

Some dreamers understand that they must improve their lives to achieve their goals. Self-improvement becomes a need rather than a choice. Dreamers understand that they cannot achieve their goals by repeating the same actions and expecting different results. Rather than staying on the same route and falling behind, they must improve and move forward.

However, if you do not dream and see a better life for yourself, one filled with abundance. You will continue to exist in a condition of scarcity, enslaved by bad habits and a seemingly unchanging status quo. As a result, when you dream, you become aware of the limitless possibilities of achieving your goals, which leads to change.

We will not be able to achieve our goals until we change. That is the fact that dreamers are aware of. However, it takes a certain kind of dreamer. One can realise their full potential to make dreams a reality. It is not brain surgery, but it does need a persistent effort to follow through day after day and not make excuses.

If you are a dreamer with some ruthless ambitions in mind, then set out on a journey of self-improvement. Develop a set of positive habits, create an empowering morning routine, and kick the negative behaviours out of your life. If you want to achieve your goals, it is not enough to imagine a better life. It will help if you take action to make it a reality.

**#5 You can recover faster if you fail.**

Failure is an unpleasant experience. I have been there much too often. Those failures, on the other hand, have aided rather than harmed me. I did not understand it at the time, but those mistakes ended up being beneficial to me in the long term. Mentally, spiritually, emotionally, I grew up. I was in physical discomfort, but I came out on top metaphysically.

Something hurts us so much when we go through a failed period that it is almost impossible to see the forest through the trees. We could not care less about how it is meant to benefit our lives in the long run when we are in the middle of it. However, it does. Moreover, as a dreamer, you have probably failed before. You will probably fail again. That is fine, in any case.

Ordinary people take longer to recover from failure than dreamers. Why? Because they have huge dreams. They pick themselves up, brush themselves off, and attempt it again when the primary upset and agony has passed. Moreover, the truly dedicated dreamers will keep trying until they reach their lofty goals, no matter how difficult it may be.

The truth is that when you fail, you tend to reflect. Nevertheless, when you achieve, you prefer to celebrate. On the other hand, failure fosters the abilities needed for long-term success. It is not simply the transient type that we can experience with momentary (but fast fading) emotions of bliss.

Do not be scared to dream because you could fail. It will help you develop character and equip you with the tools you need to achieve in the long run.

## #6 Manage your time more successfully.

While you cannot believe that the dreamers are influential time managers, those serious about accomplishing their goals are. There are no limits to what you can accomplish if you can efficiently manage your time. However, if you are prone to becoming side-tracked, reaching your goals may be more difficult or strenuous.

People who are serious about their aspirations need to be able to manage their time well. Even if you can vividly visualize your dreams and what your life would be like if they came true, turning them into reality is significantly more difficult without consistent activity within the context of an effective time-management strategy.

Our most valuable resource is time. It is the same amount for everyone because there are only 24 hours in a day. No one has more time than the other. It is essentially the greatest equalizer in life. But what changes is how we spend what little time we have. Do we squander it? Or do we effectively leverage it to attain our goals?

That makes a significant impact. If you are serious about your objectives, you already know the importance of an effective time management strategy. It is entirely up to you whether you utilize the quadrant time management system or another. The important thing is that you pick anything and ensure that your precious hours, minutes and seconds are not wasted.

### #7 The term "impossible" no longer applies to you.

You ignore the word impossible as a dreamer. Indeed, the word impossible communicates to you, "I am Possible."

When you can vividly imagine anything, anything is conceivable.

Other people may try to convince you not to pursue your aspirations, but you will not listen to them. You are a fantasist. You have got a crazed look on your face. Whatever it takes, you are going to achieve your goals.

We dreamers do not notice the bumps in the road. We are blind to the stumbling hurdles. We also overlook our previous failures. We keep moving forward, chasing our aspirations. We do not give up, and we certainly do not stop. We may have significant setbacks and fail numerous times. Nevertheless, we pick ourselves up and try again and again until we achieve our goals.

That is what it means to be a dreamer. There is nothing impossible. It is possible to achieve anything. You can nearly taste it because you can see it so clearly and vividly. Moreover, that is a part of the fight. That is what it is like to be a dreamer.

## #8 You start looking for motivation from people who have achieved.

Dreamers can achieve their goals by following in the footsteps of those who have gone before them. When you have a dream so vivid in your mind that it feels almost natural, you are looking for ways to carry it out. Furthermore, we frequently look to those who motivate us to do so. We look to those who have not only fought but also won battles.

It is never easy to follow your aspirations. Nevertheless, it seems a little less daunting when looking at others who have accomplished great goals despite seemingly insurmountable odds. How do they pull it off? How do you go about it, and what are their thoughts? What difficulties did they have to overcome? Moreover, how did they manage to pull it off?

You assume the role of a detective, and the crime you seek is a success. You start putting the puzzle together piece by piece. Eventually, you figure it out. Success does not seem that transitory when you seek inspiration from people who have achieved their goals while in much worse circumstances than you.

## #9 — When negative habits stifle your progress, become more aware !

One of the essential factors that hold us back from greatness is ourselves. We have the potential to be our own worst enemies. However, as a dreamer, you become more aware of these details. You become aware of the negative habits that are holding you back. You are aware of restrictive behaviours that prevent you from reaching your goals.

It does not occur immediately. This is not a procedure that happens overnight. Failure and pain, on the other hand, bring understanding and growth. Because your dreams are vital to you, you begin to pay attention to what you think, say and do daily. You learn that what you do daily affects your whole life journey.

Dealing with harmful habits is not simple. They necessitate consistent effort. When someone wants something strongly enough, they can break their poor behaviours. If your dreams are so vivid and you have compelling reasons to reach them, you will recognize that you have no other choice than to address your negative habits. They will deal with you if you do not comply.

### #10 You begin to obsess over minor details.

Dreamers obsess over the minor details. We have no other option.

As a dreamer, you realize that the little things add up. While they may not appear to be much at the time, they add up to a lot over time. That either slows us down or propels us forward. Over time, a few minutes squandered or gained here and there becomes significant. A few pounds spent or saved here and there started to matter a lot more.

You start examining the figures as well because analytics are crucial when it comes to achieving your goals. If you want to lose weight, run a successful business, or do just about anything else in life, you will need to keep track of your progress. How else would you know how far you have progressed, where you are now, and how much work you still have ahead of you? It would undoubtedly be considerably more difficult.

Even if you do not sweat the minor stuff at first as a dreamer, you will eventually. You recognize this as an essential part of the process. You cannot achieve what you want unless you plan your outcomes and evaluate what works and what does not. You can make changes early on if you recognize what is not working because you sweat the minor stuff. Moreover, eventually, you will be able to realize your grandiose ambitions.

## #11 Your tiny accomplishments add up over time.

The dreams are usually prominent in the beginning. We are not sure how we will ever get there. We consider the magnitude of the work ahead of us. However, you gradually gain tiny victories. Over time, one accomplishment after another adds up. Furthermore, over time, those victories begin to add up one by one.

This helps you gain momentum and get closer to your objectives. It is considerably more motivating to help push you just a little further when you see these things come to pass over time. We improve by week, month by month, and year by year, but we never stop because those dreams are apparent in our imaginations.

Every dreamer understands that achieving their goals will not be simple. Otherwise, they would not be worthwhile. What would be the point of doing it if everyone could do it?

No, as a dreamer, you recognize that the road ahead is long. Nevertheless, you are also willing to go the extra mile. Moreover, with time, you'll achieve and realize your goals. It is not something that happens overnight. However, in the end, it happens.

# CHAPTER TWO

## SELF-ESTEEM

## Building Your Self-esteem

### 1. Take Small Steps to Get There

Expect to learn it slowly if you have struggled with confidence for most of your life. For the time being, keep your sights set low and create achievable goals.
Recognize your strengths and concentrate on them. You will gain confidence in doing so and in knowing all of your other assets over time.

### 2. Recognize Your Weaknesses and Strengths

Low self-esteem goes hand in hand with doubting one's abilities. It's not a big deal if you are not particularly good in certain areas.
To figure out what you need to work on, learn to distinguish between your strengths and limitations. There are numerous ways to learn what you do not know these days. You will

notice an increase in your self-esteem as you become a more skilled employee.

## 3. Fake It Until It is Real

You would be shocked at how many individuals do the same thing you do with their self-esteem. This may feel like a big step if you are shy, but it is a step toward realizing how capable you are.
Faking it allows you to take more significant risks and embrace the fact that failure is inevitable.

## 4. Acknowledge and Accept Criticism

As previously stated, no one is immune to failure. Failure brings with it a slew of critics. Some people find it hard to accept criticism, even if it is meant to help them acknowledge their mistakes and improve.
Do not dwell on your failure if you want to gain confidence. Accept your error, learn from it, and constructively listen to suggestions before moving on.

## 5. Treat yourself as though you were your best friend.

You eat, sleep, and enjoy yourself because it makes you feel good. Nevertheless, you do not treat yourself the same way in words. The key is to be your own best friend, both in terms of deeds and words.

Because being too critical would only bog you down more, speak of yourself with love and respect. Celebrate your accomplishments, no matter how minor they may be.

## 6. When making decisions, trust your instincts.

When making decisions for yourself, you have undoubtedly used to consulting others. You lose sight of who you are and what you want if you do this too often. On the other hand, your intuition is there to assist you. All you have to do is listen to your gut.

Examine whether your action with this decision will result in the desired outcome and the correct thing to do. Even if it is difficult at times, believe in yourself.

## 7. Do things for yourself, not for others.

You listen to other people to gratify them at times. You will eventually make decisions for others, not for yourself. Because this is what they love and what makes them happy, which they do not.

It will help if you do things because they are enjoyable to you. If you want to boost your self-esteem, you should be aware of what you like and dislike, even if your preferences differ from those of others.

### 8. Someone will always be better than you.

Accept that there will always be those who are better than you. Never compare yourself to these people because you will always come out on the losing end. There is nothing wrong with not being better. Recognize that you have your own set of skills and talents.
If you want to be as good as other individuals in some areas, make them your inspiration instead of becoming envious of them.

It can take a long time to rebuild your self-esteem, especially if you have spent your entire life feeling inadequate. Self-esteem is essential not just for professional advancement but also for other aspects of life.

## Improving Your Self-Esteem

### Invest in your relationships.

Everybody wants to meet new friends, keep those who exist, have a robust support system and unconventional romantic connections, including you. So it is understandable if you've been urged to improve your social abilities. People with strong social skills are less lonely and are thought to be more attractive. These individuals excel at leading teams and earning more money.

According to a 20-year Stanford University research, moving from the bottom five to the top fifth in class popularity resulted in a 10% income increase. According to another research of 4,000 top CEOs, 60% of them are classic extroverts.

- Reconnect with old acquaintances (This requires less energy and yields a better return)
- Connect with super connectors (Those who know everyone)
- Always follow up.

## Everything you do should be done with love.

So, take some time to re-evaluate your goals and reorganize them around LOVE. At the same time, you keep money in mind, of course. If you are going to shoot up as many sleepless nights as possible, you should do it with a smile on your face. Love yourself like your life depends on it.

## Make big goals for yourself (in 10X)

Setting higher goals than the ones you need in the first place is the safest method to approach your future. Why? Because:

• It brings out your best qualities: You raise the bar when you have an essential juicy goal.

• You'll still get something despite your failure: You can pursue one client and succeed, or you can pursue ten clients. All of the same weight fail with six of them and succeed with the remaining four. Although a 40% rate may not appear extravagant, it is a 300 per cent boost in your compensation.

• It removes the fear of failing: The fear of failure, or FOF, can be crippling. All despise it. On the other hand, failure will mean less to you if you know that even if you fail, you'll still come up with the juice. See the previous 10-clients example. If you have ten bullets and ten targets, it is doubtful that you'll hit them all.

## Be Prepared to Fail

It is a good idea to plan for failure in all areas. Change is the one constant in life. You'll be tested more than you can imagine. So prepare yourself. Plan the setbacks before they happen, as the old Romans did (see pre-mortem Principle). You'll have more self-assurance and win more. Moreover, if the failure does occur, it will be less devastating and cruel.

## Your Life Should Be Shaped by Gratitude

Gratitude has far too many health advantages to be covered in a single book. However, you might want to emphasize how thankfulness influences our expectations. First and foremost, let us accept that you will get what you need from yourself and good or bad life.
If you believe you are unhappy, you will attract unhappiness and bad luck. If you believe you are lucky and can attract nice things into your life, you will get precisely that.

Before a hematopoietic stem cell transplant (HSCT), patients with psychosocial difficulties such as anxiety, sadness, low optimism, or a lack of social support had a higher chance of hospital readmission. They stayed longer when readmitted than those with better overall mental health.
Furthermore, research on lucky people, lottery winners, and happy 70+-year-old couples has revealed that most rely on their good fortune to maintain a cheerful outlook on life. Moreover, thankfulness is usually the source of that attitude. It will help if you live a grateful life because it makes you happy. Counting your blessings will help you realize how

fortunate and capable you are, resulting in a far brighter future.

## Empowerment builds Self-Esteem

So, what can you do to see yourself in a more positive light? How can you improve your self-esteem and your efficacy in all aspects of your life? To begin, you must adhere to three simple guidelines in your life, career, and relationships. If you follow these three easy guidelines, you will have a strong, powerful, and positive sense of self-worth...

### 1. Do it properly.

When you know what is right in your heart and do it, your self-esteem rises. "This first rule is not overly difficult. DO THE RIGHT THING. Do not do something that is not right, for you. Also, if you have any questions, consult your Bible for solutions."

Whether you call it business ethics or personal morality, you must always do the right thing. You cannot feel good about yourself if you do something you know is wrong. It is a basic guideline, even if it is not always easy to follow. "Opportunity may knock once, but temptation bangs on your front door forever," as the adage goes. As a result, select your actions carefully.

## 2. Give your all.

Accept nothing less than your very best from yourself. Do just enough to get by or turn in work that is barely good enough to fulfil the expectations and standards of your profession. It will not make you feel good about yourself. You have got to give it your best.

You will receive the rewards of tranquillity, joy, and self-esteem if you do so. It was over a century ago that "One word encapsulates the secret to job happiness: excellence. To enjoy something is to know how to do it well."

Do your best even though you will undoubtedly meet challenges. People who have high self-esteem or are attempting to improve their self-esteem find a method to get through those roadblocks.

Peter Falk was one of those people. He lost his eye because of a tumour when he was three years old. After that, he has worn a glass eye ever since. However, he did not slink about his school's back corridors with his hand over his eye, hoping no one would notice him. No, he became the president of his senior class and one of the best baseballs player in the school. When he slid into third base and was called out by the umpire,

Falk took out his glass eye and remarked, "Here, you can use another eye."

Falk went on to appear in a tiny community theatre after graduating from high school. Nevertheless, he received a call from Columbia Pictures, inviting him to travel to Hollywood for a screen test. He got his "big break." It was thrilling, but he was not signed. "For his price, I can get a two-eyed actor," an executive said. Strangely enough, no one knows what two-eyed actor Columbia Pictures chose instead. However, Peter Falk is best known for his roles on Broadway, television, and in films, for which he got two Academy Award nods.
Regardless of all his "obstacles," Falk always followed the second rule. He gave his all. Furthermore, his victory was a foregone conclusion. The same rule applies to you as well.

## 3. Treat others as you would want to be treated.

Show me someone who mistreats people. I will show you an insecure person with low self-esteem, which can seem as old-fashioned as the golden rule. You cannot feel good about yourself if you mistreat anyone. I mean anyone poorly.

How we treat people cannot help or hinder us (like housekeepers, waiters and secretaries). It reveals more about our character than how we treat essential people. Persons who are honest, kind, and fair when they have something to gain should not be mistaken with people of true character who exhibit these traits regularly, regardless of the circumstances. Character is not a showy mantle. It is who we are at our core."

You will respect yourself if you treat others with respect. George Washington Carver was well aware of this. Despite the racial hate that surrounded him, he rose to become one of the world's leading botanical scholars and one of the most recognized men of his day in the 18th and 19th centuries. This third guideline of self-esteem was central to his ideology. He explained, "No one has the right to come into this world and leave it without leaving behind him unique and acceptable reasons for having done so. Being gentle with the young, compassionate with the old, empathetic with efforts, and tolerant of the weak and powerful determines how far you can go in life. You will have been all that at a certain point in your life."

Follow these three guidelines. You'll also have a high sense of self-worth. However, you'll also receive three more advantages...

- **BENEFIT #1: You win people's trust.**

Others know they can trust you if you follow guideline #1, which is to do what is right. If you do not do what is right, others will have no reason to trust you. Many businesses have had to learn this lesson the hard way. They face a difficult, if not impossible, path ahead of them if they have done something wrong and lost their employees' faith or the general public.

- **BENEFIT #2: You win people's esteem.**

Others will instantly appreciate you if you follow rule #2, which is to do your best. However, if you slack off or try to cut corners on quality, they will lose respect for you. On the other hand, if you're a leader, you have to demand and accept nothing less than the best from others if you want their respect. Consider that for a moment. The teachers who insisted the most and got the most from you were the ones you loved the most respected.

- **BENEFIT #3: You win other people's admiration.**

When you follow rule #3, which is to treat others the way you want to be treated, others will treat you the same way. It is challenging to detest someone who likes, cares for, and treats you well.

Despite famous psychological lingo, intimidation does not work. You also do not win if you have a negative attitude like "I am either your dad or your boss. Just be quiet and listen." Lou Holtz says, "You win when you have a passion for people and treat them that way,"

## From Self-esteem to Self-Confidence

### 1. Everything will work out just fine.

Whilst self-esteem relates to how you feel about yourself, self-confidence is how you project yourself to other people, along side being intertwined with your own skills.

You are unconcerned about the outcome of social interactions if you have true self-confidence. It does not matter because you know you will be all right whatever.

### 2. Speak the truth

The truth is the truth. We will not be able to fix it. You will not be afraid of rejection if you speak confidently and honestly about yourself.

You put everything on display for everyone to see. This is your name. That is what you are good at. Furthermore, that is fine because you deserve of being treated with respect and appreciation.

## 3. Your words and actions have value.

You have worth. You, like everyone else, have the right to speak. Furthermore, you are aware of this.
If we are being honest, we are all the same. The President of the United States is also a human being. We do not know if he is insecure about something. He may experience nervousness on occasion. He is a regular guy.

We are on an equal footing. So, if you find yourself thinking about someone as more significant, meaningful, or deserving more than you are, these are your insecurities talking. You deserve it just as much as everyone else. That is something to consider.

## 4. We are all inconsequential in the grand scheme of things.

In the grand scheme of things, we are all the same. The universe will implode at some point. Everything will vanish and will fade into obscurity. Nevertheless, now that we are here, we should attempt new things and take risks. In the end, it makes no difference. So why not have a good time? Why not take a risk?

## 5. Do not be frightened.

Nothing is going to happen. You know that if you approach someone or ask a question at school, nothing terrible will happen. No one is going to kill you and hit you. It is an irrational dread. The ramifications are fictitious.

Who cares if there is a smidgeon of this obnoxious social phenomenon known as awkwardness?

Remember the first and third rules. Everything will be Okay. So, we must occasionally take risks. You are valuable.

## Boosting your self-esteem

As children, we pick up on signals and believe that we are not good enough. Illness can also dampen our spirits. As adults, however, we now can accept or reject the messages we are presented.

A combination of crucial factors results in high self-esteem. Your self-esteem will rise as you strive harder to put these things in place. Building a solid sense of self-worth does not happen overnight. It is something that happens when you do certain things and then stop doing others. If specific rules are followed, anyone can have a high level of self-esteem.

The following are the ten simple rules:

1. Quit criticizing yourself. Never say anything like "You foolish fool" or anything else insulting about yourself, no matter how bad you feel about yourself. Stop making fun of or demeaning oneself. Be compassionate, sweet and understanding.

2. Forget about comparing yourself to other people. People who are better (or worse) than you will still be around. You will never feel good if you start doing this because there will always be those who seem more confident, bright, spiritual, affluent, sexist, etc.

3. Accept praises and say "thank you" rather than "Oh, that was nothing." Stop rejecting compliments. You are deserving of praise, and others like offering them as much as you should enjoy receiving them.

4. Repeat positive affirmations every day. For instance, repeating phrases like "I am a useful and worthwhile individual with my own beliefs and opinions." Believe in yourself as much as you believe in your thoughts and beliefs.

5. Read on self-esteem development whenever possible. Make it your life's work. Realize that it will always be a "work in progress. Even if you find only one thing that concerns you after reading a book about self-esteem, the money you have spent will have been well spent.

6. Surround yourself with positive people and avoid negative individuals. They are destabilizers, not builders of trust. With the right conditions, just like the flower flourishes with the right fertilizer and conditions, you will grow in confidence and esteem.

7. Keep a positive journal in which you record all of your accomplishments, no matter how minor. This list should be read regularly. Close your eyes and feel your triumph all over your body.

8. Spend time on activities you love and are passionate about. Do whatever makes you happy. Give some of your time to others and assist them. Remember to give of yourself because you are cultivating wealth and positivity.

9. Always act on what you stand for. Live the life you want, not the life they said you should have. The only person you need to ask for permission is yourself.

10. Always remember that you are a magnificent human being who can make a positive difference in the world. This is your right as a child. You are indeed one-of-a-kind, deserving of love, and capable of giving love to others. Feel good about yourself and respect yourself.

# CHAPTER THREE

## FOCUS ON YOURSELF

## For a Successful and Fulfilling Life

### 1. Have faith in yourself yet recognize your limitations.

The first step to reaching all your goals and realizing that you aspire to recognize that you are human:

You are not flawless. You cannot accomplish everything on your own.

Always keep things in perspective. Do not put yourself under so much stress that you cannot move. Trust yourself to get the job done, but also be willing to give yourself some leeway.

When you make a mistake, own up to it. Set objectives and take pleasure in the trip.

## 2. Simplify and de-clutter

A thousand things are vying for your attention:

You have to clean the kids' rooms again, wash the dishes and laundry, and deal with the never-ending domestic tasks. You must organize your calendar to make a place for extra appointments, set aside time to socialize, assist your children with their schoolwork, and run a billion school runs.

Do not even begin to think about what needs to be done at work.

Let us be clear not to accomplish anything unless you gain some of the clarity that comes with making space in your life, relationships, and surroundings.

It is only by reducing and streamlining that you will stop feeling overwhelmed and pressured.

Donate anything you have not used in the last three years. Make a plan.

Enjoy the principle of appreciating without obtaining and enjoying without owing.

## 3. Everything should be used in moderation.

Adopt the "having enough" philosophy:

There is no need to go to extremes. So use caution and learn to control any compulsive tendencies.

You should spend less money than you earn. Keep an eye on your nutrition and watch less television.

## 4. Maintain a sense of perspective

Recognize that there will be times when nothing goes your way. You'll spend your days fighting conflicts, solving difficulties, and limiting damage.

We have all had such days. It is all too easy to become engrossed in the drama. Gather your wits. This, too, shall pass.

Your child will improve soon. The loud neighbourhood parties will stop, your backstabbing colleague will be transferred (we can dream, can't we?). There will be days when you can cross everything off your to-do list.

Do not get too worked up about minor details. Maintain an open mind.

## 5. Be attentive to the need of others.

If you try to treat others the way you want to be treated instead of how they want to be treated, you may have problems.

For example, if you are not a phone person, you may avoid calling your friend because you believe they share your feelings, which may not be the truth.

Try to be attentive to the needs of others. Go out of your way to help them on occasion.

Try not to pass judgment. Be generous; regularly, attempt to do something pleasant for someone.

## 6. Prioritize your family.

That is not to say that my work is not essential. It just means that I need to work in a convenient method for my family and me.

How important is it to be with your family? Do you ensure that your work is not detrimental to your work? What are your plans to get there?

You do not have to stop living your life for your family, but prioritizing and making time for them will help you feel less guilty.

## 7. Pay attention to what is going on right now.

Stop worrying about what has happened in the past or what may happen in the future.

Learn to savour each moment by living in the moment. Try mindfulness meditation.

## 8. Maintain a positive outlook

All-day long, you are what you think.

If all you have are negative thoughts rushing through your mind, that is precisely what you will receive. So try to adopt a more positive view of life.

You'll be surprised how quickly everything you hope will emerge in your surroundings.

"Whether you believe you can or believe you cannot, you are correct." Henry Ford was a famous American businessman.

## 9. Continue your education.

People interested in life and never lose their "beginner's mind" are the most interesting. They seek out new experiences and continue to develop personally and professionally.

Be a lifelong student. To be intelligent, you do not have to be old.
It will help if you read good books. Each day, try and learn something new. Take classes on subjects you're interested in.

## 10. Have a strong desire for something.

Some people have so much energy and life that others are drawn to them and feel driven to listen to them.

If you ask a passionate home cook, aspiring interior designer, gourmet chocolate connoisseur, or antique collector a question about their passion, they will speak your ear off.

You aspire to be that individual:

Someone enamoured with something remarkable.

Have one significant hobby that motivates you to pursue your passion. You will look forward to something unique every day.

## 11. Be contemplative at all times

**Do you ever think about yourself when you're alone?**

What makes you feel this way? What is it that makes you tick? What irritates you the most? What kind of things do you fantasize about? What are you unable to overcome? What are some of your last regrets?

Spend some time thinking about those topics. Then you will gain a better understanding of yourself. You would be shocked how much such reflection may change your life.

To gain a thorough understanding of yourself, consider taking a Myers-Briggs Type Indicator (MBTI) or another personality test.

## 12. Surround yourself with encouraging individuals.

Friends, literature, and your minds are three things that can make your life better.
Select them carefully.

Stay away from doubters and party poopers.

## 13. Remove the word "perfection" from your vocabulary.

Pay attention to what you tell your kids. Always do your best, and ignore the rest.

You are an expert in your field. Aim for excellence rather than perfection.

## 14. Either fix it or cope with it, but do not complain about it.

Nobody loves someone who constantly complains.

If you look around, you will notice many folks who have been dealt a lousy hand but are managing to make the best of it.

Do not point the finger at others for your troubles. Make no apologies. Do not let your emotions get the best of you. Do not be a diva when it comes to drama.

## 15. Make a list of things for which you are grateful.

Try the following exercise:

Make a list of everything that makes you happy, joyful, and appreciative whenever you feel down.

It may be a lovely family, adorable children, friendly friends, good health, a happy home, a job that covers the bills, a surprise supper served by a loving husband, a blog, favourite books and keepsakes, and an unexpected £20 money in your trouser pocket.

Everything matters.

Consider what happened to your sentiments of doom and gloom after you have done this.

It is tough not to feel uplifted after thinking about all the beautiful things you have in your life.

Always be thankful, and make room for more enjoyment.

## 16. It is possible to have it all, but not all at the same time.

This is the furthest thing from the truth:

It is impossible to have everything at the same time. You only may have 24 hours in a day and must prioritize your relationships, job, and spiritual well-being.

The focus can change on any given day. Your kids have to attend extracurricular care on certain days because you have an important meeting. Nevertheless, work must take a back seat on other days due to a sick child with a high fever.

You need to chill with your girls now and again because it has been a long time since you last took a vacation.

Life does not have to be complicated. You do not have to do everything all at once.

# How Do They Become Successful ?

**1. They create objectives and stick to them.**
Setting a goal is one thing. Achieving that objective is quite another. Almost everyone makes objectives, but only a few people have the courage and discipline to stick to them. We all make resolutions to what we would like to start or stop doing at the beginning of each year. Can you confidently state that you have accomplished 40% of your goals since the beginning of the year? You will succeed if you follow this guideline. You will remain a local champion if you do not.

**2. They are dependable.**
While some scientists may not agree with that principle completely, it contains more truth than lies. It will help if you remain constant to become genuinely outstanding at whatever it is you do. Take advantage of every chance you get to do what you love and do it effectively. It is a secret that everyone who succeeds knows.

**3. They make the best of all circumstances.**
If you want to be successful, you must be prepared and capable of making the best of any situation because difficult times will undoubtedly arise.

**4. They accept personal accountability for their actions.**
Nothing happens to us by accident. Our current lives reflect our previous choices. The actions we make now will affect our future. In the film, you can tell that he refused to accept his situation despite his lousy upbringing. He accepted responsibility for his actions and resolved to make a difference in the world. He made the best of what he had to get what he desired.


**5. They establish beneficial ties.**
You will need others to assist you to attain your goals. You will not be able to do it alone because you need mentors, partners, employees, and a spouse, among other things. Compatibility, experience, comparable beliefs, loyalty, and mutual gain are just a few factors for selecting effective partners and mentors.


**6. They make extraordinary sacrifices.**
Sacrifice is needed to achieve greatness. It is proportional to their goal. They work hard, do not waste time, always have the ultimate goal in mind. Never give in to unreasonable short term gratification.

### 7. They are never defeated.
We'd probably still be in the dark right now if he had not given up. The test of time is the most challenging card life has dealt you and me. This test will only be passed by those who are resilient and determined to persevere.

### 8. They are willing to take chances.
Every successful man or woman takes calculated risks. Our lives were formed by society and those closest to us when we were kids. For instance, your parents probably told you to go to school, get secondary grades, and get a great job. Everything our culture preaches to us is to gain stability, which is why you get terrified whenever you want to make a significant life decision or do anything out of the ordinary. The difference between a successful person and a failure is that successful people run to their anxieties, while failures escape. "Every day, do something that scares you." You will never grow if you do not follow these tips, and you may forget to be successful.

### 9. They place a high value on hard effort and discipline.
To be successful in life, you must discover something you enjoy doing and put your heart and soul into it. "There is nothing worthy that you cannot do with faith, discipline, and unselfish devotion," Muhammad Ali stated.

**10. They add worth to the world.**
Wealth and attention are attracted to value. Solving a problem is the simplest definition of success. Find a problem that your skills, passion, dreams and potential are all programmed to solve and then work on them. Pizza delivery was born due to the rising demand for pizza and the desire for easier and faster access to pizza. Businessmen and women needed a faster way to get to business meetings all over the world. Therefore the private jet was born. You were created to address a specific problem. Solve that challenge, and you will be successful.

The preceding suggestions are merely guidelines that will not lead to success until you decide to make them a habit. Nothing will be able to stop you if you decide to succeed now.

## Rules That Will Help YOU Succeed

1. Be honest with yourself. Even if your mother knew all of your worst experiences, live in such a way that she would be proud of you. No one is without flaws. We all make errors. We are all going to fall. We should, however, constantly endeavour to do the right thing and do our best to live a life of integrity. Integrity to me means doing the right thing even when no one is looking.

2. Do something that lights your spirit on fire. If there is one thing I have learned about life, the rest of the world is incorrect. Happiness is not a result of success. Success is a result of happiness. When we follow our hearts, we are joyful. We are most alive and naturally willing to give 100 per cent to every minute of every day when we are at our happiest. Extraordinary things can happen when we give our all to every minute of every day. Dreams can become a reality. Do whatever it is that enlivens your spirit. We do not get to pick who or what we love in life, which is ironic. Regardless of logic or explanation, our hearts want what our hearts want. It is an indication of when you have a strong attraction to someone or something. Accept it (as long it is not harming anyone or making you do anything illegal or immoral). The world does not require any more people who are obsessed with material possessions. No, it takes more people to live to make the world a better place for everybody.

3. Look for role models and mentors. Success leaves a trail. Look for mentors and role models who have already accomplished what you want in life. Study what the happiest couples have done to stay together for decades if you want true love. Suppose your ambition is to become the finest lawyer in your country. Research the best lawyers in your city or country how they built their reputations. If you want to be a World Champion, understand how they accomplished it by studying the lives of World Champions. Find wealthy role

models whom you aspire to be someday if you want to be a millionaire. Find a few entrepreneurs who inspire you and study how they did what they did if you want to be an entrepreneur. Mentors and role models are your shortcuts to realizing your full potential in life. You will boost your chances of success and avoid making costly blunders if you learn from others' mistakes. History is a terrific teacher when it comes to knowing what to do and what not to do.

4. Increase your growth by 1% per day. Each of us is a work in process. No one is without flaws. The essential thing is to continue to learn, grow, and evolve daily. Compounding is one of the most potent forces in the universe. If you increase the value of something by 1% every day for 70 days, it will double in value. It's impossible to say whether you're going up to 1% a day, 0.1% a day, 5% a day, or not at all. Simply put, we should all endeavour to learn, grow, and change daily. It is a way of life. It is a way of thinking that people regularly have. It is a philosophy of life. Make every effort to learn from your experiences, books, seminars, films, conferences, history, and other sources. Every day is a chance to improve as a father, son, brother, mother, daughter, sister, doctor, engineer, fighter, entrepreneur, student, or anything you want to be.

5. Surround yourself with brilliance to help you reach your full potential. We are all just the average of the five persons

we spend the most time with. You will become a dreamer and achiever if you surround yourself with dreamers and achievers. You will become a hater and a doubter if haters and doubters surround you.

6. Accept failure. As already previously mentioned, failures are nothing more than stepping stones on the road to success. Make use of them as opportunities to learn, grow, and progress. In truth, many of the world's most successful people have stories and stories of failure before they became great. Your secret to success is a failure.

7. You should give more than you take. It is not always altruistic but rather a long-term relationship strategy. You will always find yourself in favourable positions if you create win-win scenarios and leave some value to the other side. If you do the opposite, you will constantly end up in an adverse scenario. Gratitude attracts people naturally. Greed has a natural aversion to it. The average person is interested in what he can get from the world. The amazing man looks for ways to give back to the world. I am a firm believer in this adage. I make every effort to live up to it.

8. Get rid of the rotten apples. Nothing is more damaging in life than having negative, selfish, entitled people in your life. It takes courage and strength to get rid of the bad apples in your life, but it is essential to reach your full potential.

Consider those individuals to be dead weight bricks. Cut the deadweight bricks out of your life and watch it soar.

9. Opt for brightness above the darkness. Every day, every one of us is fighting a battle within ourselves. Do not give in to feelings of rage, greed, laziness, jealousy, hatred, revenge, arrogance, entitlement, or any other unpleasant emotion. Believe it or not, negative energy breeds more negative energy. Living in a hostile environment will attract complainers, whiners, doubters, and detractors. Choose positive energies like gratitude, humility, patience, courage, happiness, hard work, generosity, and kindness wherever possible. It does not imply that we must all live in the light with positive energy at all times of the day. No, it would be impossible because, after all, we are all human. However, I make every effort to choose brightness over darkness every day. Goodness and positivity, like evil and negativity, are choices. Be aware of what you eat every day. Whatever you eat will be you.

10. Have a warrior's spirit. Be impenetrable. Things will go wrong for all of us. It is simply a fact of life. Life is not always kind. Some of us will be bereft of a loved one far too soon. Some of us will develop health issues. Some of us will have to deal with poverty. Unfortunate events will strike some of us. Promise yourself that you will always do your best and fight the good fight no matter what happens in your life. Be

a fighter. It does not matter how many times you fall in life. What matters is that you always get back up to pursue your goals.

This list reflects only my personal experiences, beliefs and ideals. It may or may not apply to you, but this is by no means a comprehensive list. That being said, these ten guiding concepts and values have been highly beneficial to me throughout my life. I hope that at least a few of them will be beneficial to you as well. Make a positive impact. Live your passion. Never, ever quit up. May the quest of your life to discover your grandeur to be joyful and rewarding!

# What You Think Becomes Your Reality #2

A fundamental aspect of attaining our deepest wants and dreams is the existence of a general and unshakeable belief that we can achieve anything we want in life. One of the most critical determining variables in our ability to acquire or achieve something is our belief, faith, or the unconscionable certainty that we are meant to do so.

The majority of the time, we doubt ourselves. We live in a perpetual state of fear, anxiety, tension, and worry, stressing and overthinking every action, unsure if it will ever be good enough to achieve our goals and live the life we deserve. This occurs considerably more frequently in our lives than having complete faith in ourselves.

Nevertheless, don't we all have reasons for overthinking things, continuously fretting, and living in fear? When so many things are at stake, how are we expected to take the significant risks that come with huge rewards? What happens if we fail? What if we cannot provide for our family, keep a roof over our heads, or feed ourselves?

However, that is all there is to it. Fears are pretty easy to materialize. When the mind gets rolling, it can spiral out of control. This is something that many of us are all too familiar with. The mind is a potent weapon that may be utilized for good or can certainly be used for evil. As the adage goes, like attracts like.

So, if you want to do anything in life, you must have complete control over that immensely complicated bundle of tissue and substance in your skull known as your brain, as well as the construct that sits within it, known as your mind.

## YOU, Creating Your Future Reality Through Thinking

Our subconscious mind processes multiple thoughts and ideas all day. Those same ideas pull us towards anything we want while bringing us closer to the things we dread. The complexity of our thoughts and the three-part interaction in the psychic apparatus, the mind's driver, can be disorienting.

How can we accomplish anything when our minds seem to be fighting against us? The truth is that we get whatever we focus on in life. We already know deep down inside. We get the same when we dwell on negative thoughts like fear, wrath, and resentment. Honestly, we live in a perpetual feeling of scarcity, wondering why we do not seem to get the things we so desperately desire in life.

We gain more of the same when we live an abundant life, rooted in positivity, moving away from fear, anger and resentment towards love, development, contribution and forgiveness. What attracts like attracts like. It is pretty plain and easy to understand. However, we rarely see it on a micro-level. We tend to view things on a larger scale, oblivious to what is happening in the present moment.

So if you want to achieve these lofty goals that you have set for yourself, live a rich life and grow spiritually, commit yourself to follow three simple guidelines. Moreover, as corny as it may sound, there are three easy guidelines to follow to achieve anything you desire in life.

However, do not get me wrong. This is not a quick-fix solution. It is not a bandage that you can put on and expect old wounds to heal and your life to be changed before your eyes. It will help if you delved more profound than the surface. It will help if you get to the root of whom you are as an individual acting within the limits of society, despite all of the hardship. What do you intend to offer to the table?

Delivering value is the key to success in life, no matter what field we are talking about. Whoever adds the most value to the world will be able to attain anything they desire. People may skim over this simple fact, but it should be ignored. Do not look for shortcuts or underhanded techniques that will help you develop at the expense of others. Commit to living a value-driven life.

Overall, these three simple guidelines for attaining everything you want out of life may seem simple enough. However, practicing them daily, without fail, is the tricky part. We have all experienced how life can get in the way. However, just as nothing great in life comes easily, do not anticipate accomplishing a lofty objective to be simple.

This is the tricky part. That is where many folks lose interest and concentrate. Big ambitions necessitate much effort. It is not going to happen in a day or two. We have evolved into an on-demand society that expects everything to be delivered quickly. Reaching huge goals is not nearly that simple.

However, if you're ready to put in the effort and not give up, you can achieve anything in life. As far-fetched as a significant objective may appear today, you move closer to it. The reality of it becomes apparent.

## #1 — Have a clear understanding of what you want and why you want it.

You should know what you want and why you desire it. It is the first easy guideline in attaining anything in life. While this may appear to be a simple concept, it is at the centre of all achievement. It entails being explicit about your objectives and writing them out in great detail. It also necessitates having a compelling cause for desiring what you desire in the first place.

Numerous studies have found that neither clear nor stated goals are significantly less likely to be met. Setting passive targets is included in these kinds of targets. Passive goal-setting is significantly more arbitrary and non-committal than active goal-setting. So, if you're serious about accomplishing something significant, you will need to set goals actively.

Knowing exactly what you want out of life is quite powerful. It guides, encourages and motivates you on the correct route. It establishes a framework. It also provides a strong sense of purpose. Knowing exactly what you want, right down to the smallest detail, is the key to making your goals a reality. It is the first part of the equation.

When we are crystal clear on what we want, you may call it the Law of Attraction, destiny, or just goal setting. There is a robust pool of vibrational energy that we cannot see. It binds and pulls us in the right direction. Make it exact and genuine. Make it specific and quantifiable. Using the SMARTER technique, you may appropriately set your goals. This is the first step toward achieving your goals in life.

However, make sure you understand why you desire what you want. If that reason is strong enough, it can provide you with the motivation to persevere. It will not support you in times of need if it is fragile or artificial. That deep-enough motive for achievement will enable you to see your goals through when you are feeling down, anxious, or worried about whatever it is.

## #2 — Make and stick to a large-scale action plan.

As cliché as it may sound, one of the most significant impediments to most of us accomplishing our goals is the need to take concrete action regularly. While it appears to be straightforward, we all know that it is far from the case. Many of us have experienced first-hand how difficult it is to keep taking action daily and push past the barriers that hold us back.

Nevertheless, that is exactly what is required. You have covered the first step if you know what you want and why you want it. It's strong enough to motivate you to achieve it. Nevertheless, it is not the complete picture. It will help if you design a comprehensive action plan.

Consider the flight of an aeroplane for a moment. An aeroplane has a destination in mind. It knows where it is headed and why it is flying there. For example, a plane flying from London Heathrow Airport (LHR) to John F. Kennedy International Airport (JKF) in New York knows exactly what it wants. It wants to fly from LHR to JFK for a reason. It understands why people are paying for the service.

The plane also has a large-scale action plan. This is referred to as the flight plan in the case of an aeroplane. The starting location and destination are known in the flight plan. It also knows things like the overall direction of travel, the average flying altitude, and the cruise speed, among other things. Some elements influence the flight plan.

How would the plane know how to travel from Point A to Point B if it did not have a flight plan? How could it go from LHR to JFK without all the intricacies worked out? Those intricacies are the amount of jet fuel needed, the aircraft's weight with all its contents, like passengers, crew and luggage, and other factors?

Even if an aircraft does not know what it wants and why it wants to do it, it will be complicated. Similarly, you will need a plan to accomplish anything you want in life. Otherwise, you will be wasting your time if you do not know how to travel from one location to the next. Obtaining anything you desire in life becomes significantly more difficult without this information.

## #3 — Keep track of and analyse your outcomes, making adjustments as needed.

The third easy rule for achieving anything in life is to keep track of and analyse your progress while making adjustments as needed. Consider that aeroplane for a moment more. It has a comprehensive action plan in place to get there. However, what happens if there is turbulence along the way. Or if there is significant air traffic congestion or another problem?

Is the plane going to come to a halt and turn around to return home? Or does it continue, making modifications as it goes? We are all aware of the solution. However, the aeroplane can only make those adjustments if it is tracking and interpreting its data. An aeroplane monitors everything down to the last second on a micro-scale. The onboard computers assist in crunching the data and devising alternate plans when needed.

Similarly, if you want to achieve anything in life, you must keep a thorough track of your progress and analyse your results along the way. How else could you tell if you have gone off the rails? If an aeroplane fails to track its flight path for an hour, it may end up flying in the wrong direction, squandering fuel, and causing inconvenience to its passengers.

If you want to attain your objectives, you must meticulously track and analyse your progress. Data is what you live and breathe. Examine it. Obsess about it. Determine how you can improve the data and help to improve things incrementally. If you want to save £20,000 to start a business, for example, you'll need to get serious about your income and expenses.

You will need to track your costs down to the last cent to save £20,000. Every pound you spend is a pound that is not going towards your goal. As a result, if you buy a pack of gum, keep track of it. Keep track of your morning latte. Then go through your findings with a fine-toothed comb. How much of your income is spent on "extras" in your life? How much of the budget is allocated to the necessities?

People may overlook the nuances, yet those same elements will help you reach your goals in life. If you want to see things through, you must become detailed even if you are not already. No one else will be able to help you.

While these guidelines appear basic at first glance, they include an entirely different way of thinking and living. The more we stray from our path, the less likely we will fulfil the goals we set for ourselves. Take them seriously and commit to devoting the time and effort required to complete the task. This way, you'll be able to attain even the most ambitious goals you set for yourself. Just do not hold your breath for it to happen right now.

## Yourself in a Better Position for Success

It takes more than luck to succeed in business. It takes a lot of guts and big-picture thinking, as well as the determination to overcome the concerns that keep you locked, accepting smaller rewards.

Work on reducing the barriers of small-mindedness, conformity, and self-imposed constraints to raise success standards dramatically. Set high expectations for yourself and never apologize for them. People who want to work for and with you will go above and beyond to fulfil your highest standards.

Your work ethics, personal development, and responsibilities set the tone for your life and career. Remember to think big, expect nothing less than the best, have bravery. Above all, be enjoyable as you follow the seven guidelines below.

**1. Work together with others.**

Relationships are at the heart of success. Customers and co-workers should be involved in the design and direction of your company's goals. You should set expectations for the work to be performed in your area of responsibility with each individual. Make those requirements difficult but achievable. As a result, you'll be able to achieve the high levels of productivity and service that you desire.

In business, you can only get so far on your own. To be successful, empowered and fulfilled, you need the help of others. Choose your goals and empower your team to get your company where it needs to go into business, rewarding team members along the way.

## 2. Do not be oblivious.

In the pursuit of success, personal power and complacency cannot coexist. Make time and effort to ensure that no vital areas of attention, whether personal or professional, are overlooked.

Complete jobs and responsibilities. Work hard to overcome challenges, focusing on what you can gain, learn, and improve to make life and business more smoothly. Make a list of items that need to be done, together with performance objectives and completion dates. Concentrate your attention on what matters most in the long run rather than what is urgent. Urgency causes the mind to become irrational. Allow those components to settle before concentrating on what you can manage.

## 3. Consider opportunities rather than issues.

With personal strength, you have the conviction that there are solutions to difficulties. Instead of getting stuck in incorrect assumptions about why things cannot be done, approach problems from a solution-focused viewpoint. Engages the creative process of investigating and architecting alternate routes.

If you cannot develop a solution, share your views with others and ask for their opinions and suggestions. Solution-oriented minds encourage and reward one another. When you concentrate on finding answers, you learn to fail and adapt rather than fix and fail.

**4. Do a self-review.**

To increase your power, adopt the motivational mindset of constantly monitoring, reviewing, and altering your work. Attitude and beliefs to avoid complacency and continue to reach your higher goals.

Writing things down and defining your course is one of the most effective techniques to keep yourself motivated in obtaining your more meaningful goals. Describe what exceptional performance would look like in light of your goals. Then what complacent performance would look like, along with specific plans to avoid lower-level habits.

Setting performance criteria midway between complacency and superiority is what personal power entails.

## 5. Keep track of your time.

The power of the present moment looks at where you spend most of your time maintaining your authority. Do you prioritize the most critical chores first, or do you tend to prioritize the small, tiresome jobs that appear to be more urgent? Getting wrapped up in little, pressing chores diverts your attention away from the more essential goals that require your attention. Concentrate on the most significant issues and proceed from there.

When it comes to your connections, always arrive on time or early for all business. Professional activities, as this gives your obligations a sense of importance. This is power when you can make someone else feel important. How you manage your time reveals a lot about your dedication and character as a person and a leader.

You and everyone around you will work to much better standards if you respect your time and others'.

## 6. Take ownership of your actions.

Whatever occurs in your life or profession, accept responsibility for the results of your efforts, both positive and negative. It is the most passable road to developing your power. If you make a mistake, consider it a self-created learning opportunity to determine what needs to change your efforts to be more effective. Accepting responsibility helps you to be adaptable and adjust your strategy.

Understand that mistakes give more than they come to power. All new directions emerge from mistakes.

It is not about ego when it comes to effective leadership. It all boils down to humility and an eagerness to learn. Inspire others to take personal responsibility for their work's outcomes. You must first model these habits openly, powerfully and continue to instil them in others.

The gift your particular strength inspires is elevating another person to a more significant state of existence.

## 7. Be considerate.

As a human being, there is no higher value than the absolute power of kindness. Kindness does not imply that you are a pushover or a "yes" person. A kindness that generates success is the kind of kindness that can convey both good and bad news gracefully. The kind of kindness that delivers feedback rather than criticism is directed toward more significant standards. A kindness that motivates people to work hard is kindness that sees potential rather than issues.

Kindness is important. Treat yourself and the people you work with and for respectfully. Create an emotional atmosphere that is infectious, contagious, and beneficial to everyone fortunate enough to be a part of it. More than any other human quality, kindness will propel you forward in life.

To embrace your inherent freedom to think independently, speak your mind, pursue happiness, success, and financial gain. Seek inner awareness and a sense of serenity. To do so without having to submit to the mean spirited norms of anyone else, including yours, is to have and lead personal power. By being yourself, you can empower yourself. Use your opportunities, plan your goals, lead with kindness. Aim for that beautiful and attainable sense of personal independence.

## From Those Who Know What They are Doing

### 1. Concentrate on the process rather than the outcome.

Having a long term goal is a normal part of life, usually it changes along the way, depending on our experiences, but the core of it will always involves, love, wealth, health, success and comfort. Having that in mind try to focus on which of the previous will your outcome provides you, concentrate on it during the process, think about the details, why not try to make the journey as enjoyable as the outcome? After all, you may spend more time battling through the objectives then at the outcome. Enjoy the present, soon the "outcome" will become it!

## 2. Pay Attention — In What Matters

Giving up on our plans to help a friend or even a stranger, we have all done it, "why not ?", "it can wait" we say. It is very easy to get carried away by the satisfaction, you can then go and tell everyone how much of a good person you are. There is nothing wrong with this, but be aware, soon you could be wasting your time.

Focus on yourself and what matters to you, this should be your main priority, keeping your friends close, under your radar. Help everyone when possible.

## 3. Put what you want to get out and maybe a little more.

Hard working doesn't necessarily means constantly feeling exhausted, keeping focus of you want to achieve all the time can also be very emotionally draining. Occasionally planting seeds of relaxation will soon become a very tasty reward, "you reap what you sow", they say. Anything that brings you joy and place you closer to your goal is welcome. Determination to succeed is essential to you not anyone else.

## 4. Make the most of your assets. Do not be embarrassed by your flaws.

If you would ask a famous painter to perform brain surgery he would very likely be unwilling to even try. We are all born with a unique set of skills. Be proud of what you're good at.

Your difficulties help you to build your strengths, "character building exercise" so I was told, but it takes strength to persevere in the face of adversity, never give up.

## 5. Gratitude Is Required

Practice gratitude often, against or odds, when no one else will, the more you can repeat this act the more neurological connections you'll create in your brain, the moment this experience encounters emotion a stronger chemical connection between your mind and body will be created, even changing your genes, now whenever you think about your future, the chemical reactions will be exactly like those from your past, to the extent that your future will feel like it already happened, now your mind and body are both well connected towards the one positive outcome.

Gratitude can transforms what we have into more than enough. It transforms rejection into acceptance, disorders into order, and ambiguity into clarity. It has the power to transform a meal into a feast, a house into a home, and a stranger into a friend.

## 6. Keep in mind that INSTINCT is NOT the same as an IMPULSE.

**Impulse** guides us towards something we seek (often pleasurable).
**Instinct** is a sense towards something that is challenging your welfare or values.
**Intuition** is the control between impulse and instincts, moderating both.
**Inspiration** is the result of a balanced mind, a vision of your thoughts and strategies, affirmation of self-governance, created by your intuition.

## 7. It is All About Simplicity

From the vast number of things happening all over the world, there is only a very small amount that you can possibly control, the Stoics call this the dichotomy of control, that is where your core energy should be focused on. What we think and how we see thing matter, the Stoics say, "life is painted with the colours of our thoughts"

"We cannot control the storm but we may be able to roll down the sails and steer the boat to safety".

## 8. Passion. It is All About Enthusiasm

As soon as we're aware that something good is about to happen our brain release chemicals known as dopamine and endorphin as well as other neurotransmitters, those send information through our brain and into it from the outside, storing information as memories, whilst dopamine and endorphin delights us, the combination of it results in learning.
It's scientifically proven that anyone will learn easier mainly by their level of enthusiasm.

Where you place your attention is where you energy will go, something exceptional will happen to you when you discipline your mind to think and focus on whatever it is that will makes you happy, two very similar positive energies starts to fuel our body, enthusiasm will fuel our short term objectives parallel to it is a more abiding energy, passion, this will guide us towards our more long term goals. Both energies are keys to leading a successful life, taking actions without passion and enthusiasm is merely give yourself a chance, you're simply going with the motion, possibly just following someone else's lead.

Enjoyment is the spark that ignites enthusiasm and passion. Focus your thoughts on the things that brings you joy.

# CHAPTER FOUR

## BUSINESS MIND

## Personal Rules

As your company grows, you'll need to stick to a set of practices that will assure your long-term success. When it comes to avoiding a potentially disastrous business blunder, having a set of rules to follow and sticking to them can make all the difference.

### Collaborate with people who have a solid moral compass.

Choose to work with people who have a solid moral compass. This is not to argue that unethical people cannot succeed in business. It just means that they will screw your customers, your culture, your employees, and eventually you when the next opportunity presents itself. You'll be too preoccupied with running a business to keep a close eye on your back. Choose those who will do the right thing in difficult situations.

## Surround yourself with the best people you can find.

You will succeed if you surround yourself daily with the most inspiring mentors, positive teams, and complete information. Running a business is challenging. So consider whom you are interacting with, what devices you are using, and what you are seeing and hearing to see if it is helping or hurting you.

## Make the Most of Your Energy

The key to building meaningful, long-term relationships is to be truthful with everyone you do business with. In any personal relationship, trust is essential. Business partnerships are no exception. Transparency with your partners, employees and clients builds the most robust foundation of trust.

The principle of "pay it forward" states that you should help others without expecting anything in return. Failure occurs in both business and life. Climbing back up each time is crucial to success. Paying it forward has enabled me to build a solid network of true lifelong friends. They have helped me in my most difficult periods and are the reason for my current achievement.

## Take the initiative and lead from the front.

Every day, spend time in the trenches with employees. Demonstrate the qualities you want to see in them (productivity, direct communication, client orientation, fun, etc.). They are considerably more inclined to follow in your footsteps rather than merely do what they are taught.

## Do it correctly or do not do it at all

This is more than a personal rule. It is the foundation of all we do as a corporation because there is no middle ground. Everyone in the organization understands that whatever we do must be done well. This provides our client's confidence in our ability to execute. Furthermore, it allows our staff to push back if anything appears to be a complete effort. It also assists us in weeding out prospects and avoiding clients who are unconcerned about quality.

## Defying all odds to find greatness.

According to the principle, you learn from your mistakes. Surprisingly, the majority of the people who have built the most successful businesses have no real market experience and even less so-called experience. Indeed, it appears that their lack of awareness of the possible risks was what allowed them to succeed. It appears that walking a high wire is considerably more manageable when you do not believe there is a 100-foot drop on either side. To put it another way, our ability to succeed is determined by our <u>belief</u> in our ability to succeed and we will not fail.

## 1. The importance of people outweighs the importance of a plan.

If you concentrate on finding individuals you want to be around and whom you believe are talented, you're more likely to develop fantastic ideas that will work together. If you start with a concept and then go for skill, you will likely end up with a square peg in a round hole. It is what Jim Collins refers to as the "who" rather than the "what". You already know those if you have read any of his works.

## 2. Understand your clients' true desires.

The value of listening to clients is taught in business school. If you know what to listen for, that is fantastic. Customers may not know what they need. Nevertheless, they may articulate what they genuinely desire or dislike. For example, people do not want to spend money on gasoline, but do want to go to the beach. Whether or not he stated that, the point is valid. Your capacity to discern what people genuinely want, not what they claim they want, determines what business you are in.

### 3. The size of the market is crucial.

When VCs consider a potential investment, they try to forecast the market. Even a half-good company can grow to be a decent size if the market is large enough. It may take ten times the effort to dominate a small market. Calculate the size of your opportunity and the portion of the market you believe you could control.

The public is a highly specialized company that assists highly specialized semiconductor and component firms with marketing. They jokingly refer to themselves as " beards." You could believe it is a small market, and you'd be right except for the fact that a specialized market is worth more than a billion pounds.

### 4. Take on the role of the customer.

How often have you witnessed employees acting against their company's best interests because its policies forced them to do so? Every year, billions of pounds are lost because people do what they are told rather than what they think they should do. You can eliminate the madness by continually putting yourself in the customer's shoes and listening to your employees.

Nobody was allowed to criticize the systems, even though everyone knew they were ridiculous.

**5. Do not go after low-quality revenue.**

You want clients while you are starting. Nevertheless, do not take just anyone's money. Some consumers can be detrimental to a company's bottom line, particularly in the services industry. If you take on customers that pay well but make your employees' lives a living nightmare, they will resign right away. You'll be out of business.

Outcast, one of the Next 15's companies, lives by this aphorism. It is in high demand due to its unwillingness to work with just anyone. In other words, it receives over a thousand new business inquiries each month. It declines the opportunity to work with customers who might potentially quadruple its annual revenues. It understands that if it dilutes its offering and works with companies that are not a good fit, the good employees will go, and the business will suffer.

**6. Be aware of your own culture.**

Businesses are similar to families in that they have a set of values and a way of life. These are frequently a result of the values of the leader or creator. As you develop, make sure to include others who share your ideals. Do not hire people who want a corner office and an assistant if your company has a relaxed and enjoyable atmosphere where people are empowered. You do not take yourself too seriously. A company's culture may make or break it. You should find out what your culture is if you do not already know it.

## 7. It's all about the timing.

Timing is one of the essential factors in determining whether a firm succeeds or fails. It is crucial to be in the right place at the right moment. All of this leads to my first argument about not being afraid of failure in life. You never know until you try. Before Google, there was a slew of alternative search engines to choose from. Do you recall Lycos? It was highly significant at the time. Then came Google. The rest, as they say, is history. Although Google did not produce a significantly better engine, it did make it at the opportune time.

## 8. Consider the possibility of expansion.

We have all fantasized about what we would do if we won the jackpot. When launching a business, consider what will happen if it becomes successful. What method will you use to scale? Whom would you hire if you had to hire someone tomorrow? Would you consider establishing a location in another city? Would you be interested in franchising the company? Do not be surprised if you crash to develop the plane while flying it.

Last but not least, do not stop innovating. If you have the proper culture (point No. 6), hire incredible people (tip No. 1), and always put yourself in your customers' shoes (tip No. 4). You have built a firm that will last. I bring up this last argument because I believe businesses have a choice: innovate or die. That is all there is to it.

Suppose we recently launched a Project, a financing program, omnipresent. We will fund the initial development of any employee's brilliant idea for a potentially viable new product, service, or business in the marketing technology space. The concept could range from product creation to starting a business. Our culture is reinforced in two ways by this ambition to innovate. It implies that we are a business that is open to big ideas from everybody. It also serves as a reminder to everyone that, even though this project is a worldwide corporation, we must think and act like a start-up. However, it might be the catalyst for the company's next phase of expansion. Markets do not remain static; they develop, and the dinosaurs are left behind.

## Great Entrepreneurs' Business Rules

There are a few things you should be aware of when it comes to rules, which leads to the question of whether rules are true.

Fact 1: Rules serve as a reference to what should and should not be done.
Fact 2: Rules aid in the preservation and extension of an organization's lifespan.
Fact 3: Rules serve to keep the entrepreneur from tampering with the activities.

Now that we understand the significance of regulations, we can respect them even more in our enterprises. The client is the sole boss, and he can fire everybody in the company, from the chairman on down, just by spending his money somewhere else. The following are the business rules: Believe in your company and put your heart and soul into it. Profits should be shared with your partners (employees). Motivate your teammates, set goals for them, and keep track of their progress. Everything should be communicated, and your spending should be kept under control. Begin small and work your way up. Concentrate on your primary business. Be sure you have a strong business concept. Make sure you are running with a vision in mind. Build your company one step at a time. Do not feel compelled to come up with a novel concept. Be ready for the worst. Never go about your everyday routine without picking up a book to read. Be truthful to yourself.

## 1. Believe in and commit to your business.

"Your determination to keep trying is the most crucial component in the failure equation." As you devote yourself to your business, your faith in it fuels your desire to keep going.

## 2. Distribute Profits to Your Partners (Employees)

Profit is one of the benefits of hard effort. If you have people working for you, the best way to keep them working for you is to share your earnings with them, i.e. your employees and partners. It contributes to the team's spirit.

## 3. Inspire your teammates, challenge them, and keep track of their progress.

One method to maintain the team's spirit up and on track to success as a business owner is to consistently motivate, challenge, and inspire them to see the best in themselves.

## 4. Make sure you communicate everything.

Business relationships with your partners, clients, consumers, and staff are significant. It will help if you express everything to them wisely. Learn the appropriate words to speak when telling them and how to tell them when communicating. Recognize the emotional state of the individual with whom you are interacting. This is one of the business rules.

## 5. Keep an eye on your spending.

This is a critical aspect of entrepreneurship to stay afloat. Ensure your cash intake exceeds your cash outflow. Make sure you do not spend more than you earn. As Warren Buffett stated, "If you acquire items you do not need, you will have to sell things you do need sooner or later."

## 6. Begin small and work your way up

Trying to sell to everyone is one of the quickest ways to fail in business, especially at an early stage. "If you want to make everyone happy, do not be a leader, sell ice cream," a wise man once advised. Instead of attempting to reach and touch everyone, the solution is to choose a speciality in which you can work at your level. As a growing firm, it is best not to be a generalist, at least not initially. It is because most small enterprises lack the resources to respond to everyone. It could be a lack of financial resources or a lack of suitable clients.

## 7. Concentrate on your primary business.

If you ask yourself what the fundamental business is, it's just the business that creates most of your revenue. Many business owners run other tiny enterprises. This is not a wrong concept, but those other businesses should not get in the way of your primary business. If you know you will be distracted if you focus on small businesses, I recommend you close them and focus on your primary business.

## 8. Make sure you have a compelling business concept.

Customers will not patronize you if they do not find value in your business, regardless of how much skill you put into it. The greatest thing to do is conduct extensive market research on what customers want. It is because developing a successful product must be done solely to gratify people, not your satisfaction.

## 9. Make sure you are pursuing your goals with a clear vision.

This is one of the business rules that you must follow as an entrepreneur or business owner. You might wonder why. There are a few reasons, but one of the most obvious is that you learn what to expect at certain times in your career. Typically, a business plan document is prepared throughout this process to put all of those visions into writing. Your competition, your market, and your strategic position in the market niche are some of the considerations when you think about it.

## 10. Build your company one step at a time.

When it comes to growing your small business, there are times when you may need to veer off in different ways. I would advise you to be very patient and wait for your current business to mature before starting a new one. This is to prevent your attention from being diverted.

## 11. Do not force the creation of a new market.

That guideline means you do not have to reinvent the wheel when coming up with ideas to build your business or start one. This is due to a variety of factors. One explanation is that growing current markets or products saves time, resources, and money, whereas trying to create a new market or product will almost always waste or consume too much time and other resources such as money.

## 12. MAKE YOURSELF READY FOR THE WORST

You do not need to be concerned about this. What this means in this context is that you have to be aware that things generally take longer and cost more than anticipated. As a result, for a smooth company flow, make sure you have a surplus rather than a deficit in terms of money, time, and other aspects.

## 13. ALWAYS READ BEFORE GOING ABOUT YOUR DAY-TO-DAY ACTIVITIES.

"Readers are leaders," says one of my favourite quotes for entrepreneurs. Because most people do not read, the secrets of a great business are generally hidden in books. Most people do not read. They struggle and strive to expand their enterprises without knowing what has to be done.

## 14. Be Honest to Yourself

If you do not enjoy the business and would not be proud to show your relatives what you are doing and how you are doing it, then do not do it. Even if you enjoy temporary success, if you run a business you don't like or believe in, it will come back to haunt you in one way or another.

## 15. Do Not Let Your Business Ownership Pass You By Your Reality Will Be Clouded By Your Dreams.

You may have wished to start your fashion firm for years. Or you may have invented a valuable new tool for removing crumbs from a toaster. Or you may have devised a service that you believe businesses would demand. Do not get too excited about your brilliant concept that you overlook information regarding the viability of the business you want to establish. Your brilliant business concept is only as excellent as the number of individuals who will be willing to pay for it.

## 16. Great products and services at a fair price.

If the difference between your cost and sale price is too small, it will be tough to expand your business. You will not be able to hire workers, pay rent (if you need to move the firm out of the house), market more, or do specific things you need to expand if your profit margins are too modest.

# CHAPTER FIVE

## BECOME DISCIPLINED...

## ...ON ACHIEVING YOUR GOALS

However, you've decided to make a significant shift this year. It will be best to do more than wish to achieve your objectives to ensure that you follow through on them. Realizing your goals will almost always necessitate a series of lifestyle modifications.

### Set goals that motivate you.

Set personal goals for yourself that will motivate you to achieve new heights. Do not go along with the pack and try to emulate your friends' objectives. Instead, pursue something you're enthusiastic about and that interests you. This can help you develop a feeling of purpose, encouraging you to stop thinking and start acting.

## Take the initiative

Life goals are things you hope to achieve 'one day,' but not today. If you want to make things happen, you need to adjust your approach. Stop looking around social media, wishing you had that career, lifestyle, and social life. Instead, get out there and do something about it.

Richard Branson, the founder of the Virgin conglomerate, has worked in business, music, journalism and politics, not to mention space exploration, philanthropy and the occasional attempt to set a world record. So it is no surprise that he has a "get up and go" attitude. The wealthy businessman has credited his success to his positive outlook on life, telling young people to "go out there and do things. Do not watch other people do things, and do not watch television." It is all too easy in today's world to take a passive approach to life, but you need to get your hands dirty if you want to accomplish important things.

## There will be no more negative.

It is true that "our attitude toward life dictates life's attitude toward us." If you project negativity out into the world, it will come back to bite you. You will not be able to do it if you tell yourself, "you cannot do this, and you cannot do that." Even if you're faking it, having a "can do" attitude, as cliché as it sounds, can genuinely help you achieve your goals. Whenever doubt creeps into your head, swat it away and remind yourself that the glass is half full.

## Maintain a healthy balance

It's easy to become fixated on setting goals. You are hooked and will go to any length to achieve your goals. However, there is a risk of burnout if you do this. From the start, be realistic about your goals. The drive is admirable, but keep in mind that you, like everyone else, require rest and restoration.

Make a schedule for yourself and allot adequate time each day or week to focus on your objective. If you want to run a 10k race, for example, your first step should be to create a training plan that includes the appropriate amount of training while avoiding weariness. Do you require assistance? To get started, look through our list of challenges.

## Take it apart

Setting and achieving goals is difficult. There are no simple options or shortcuts. But that is part of what makes the experience so fulfilling.

Break everything down if you start to feel overwhelmed not only in terms of time but also in terms of action points. Outlining what you want to do, when you want to achieve it, and how you plan to achieve it will make your goals appear much more attainable.

## Be willing to fail.

Setting goals have rarely been easy. You will run into roadblocks that make you wonder why you tried in the first place. But that is part of the process, and the sooner you embrace it, the better. Rather than let failure defeat you, accept that it has happened and learn from it. Make a list of what worked and what did not, and then move on. You will become a better goal-setter as a result of it.

## Inform everyone

The first guideline of goal-setting is to speak about it. Tell everybody who will hear about your plans and how you intend to carry them out. The increased pressure will push you to follow through on your words. Furthermore, it provides networking opportunities. Are you developing long-term company objectives? The more people you talk to, the more likely you will meet people with whom you might work and achieve your goals.

## Keep tabs on your development.

Seeing how far you've come can be a great motivator to get to the Finish Line. If your weight loss progress has come to a halt and you are tempted to revert to old (bad) habits, remind yourself of how far you have come thus far.

Take photographs, keep a diary or make a video of your goal-setting process. Keeping track of your excellent and poor weeks might also help you identify your flaws and figure out how to overcome them.

## Create a mental image of the final product.

You will be tempted to stray if you lose sight of the eventual goal. Visualizing the change, you wish to see is one of the most effective strategies to stay motivated. Make this mental image of yourself. The 'you' in X number of weeks, so you do not get warned, is more vital than ever when the inevitable setback happens.

When you achieve your goal, reward yourself. You deserve it. Have you made it around the marathon course without getting blisters? There is a beer with your name on it waiting for you after the race.

## Motivational Rules to Help You Achieve Your Life Goals

In reality, Big goals take a long time to achieve. It is not something that happens overnight. Moreover, it frequently does not occur inside the timeline that we have established. It can happen if we do not surrender to failure. Whatever you want out of life, you can achieve it if you use the proper tactics at the right moment and stick with it long enough to see it through.

The truth is that there is no simple answer. Nevertheless, there are some strategies you can employ to increase your chances of success. I have compiled a list of excellent suggestions for reaching your life goals, as recommended by some of the world's most successful people.

**Do not let rejection get in the way of your success.**

Rejection can be extremely frustrating for most, the major emotional punches usually are the feeling of disappointment that slowly affirms the reality of not getting something you hoped for, then the feeling of insecurity paralysing all intentions to even thinking about trying the same again. Despite the bitter flavour left in your mouth remember that you are fully in control of your mind, therefore your reality and future.

Take a moment to think about what was the cause of the rejection, embrace the way it makes you feel, focus on it, enable yourself to think abstractly and utilize metacognition, learn from it, soon the feeling will go and the image to what caused it becomes clearer. Remember that to succeed first we all fail, rejection is just a branch of failure. Keep trying!

**Invest in yourself.**

"The finest investment you can make is in your abilities," remarked Warren Buffet, a world-renowned businessman and philanthropist. You will be much better positioned to achieve your objectives if you constantly develop by acquiring appropriate skills and information. You only have to look at superstar footballer Cristiano Ronaldo to see how some of the world's finest athletes attribute their success to their desire to develop themselves. Although Ronaldo may not be to everyone's taste, he is one of the most dedicated players of all time, reaping the benefits of his efforts on the field regularly.

**Be willing to learn from your mistakes.**

There will undoubtedly be a few hiccups along the way to success. It will help if you do not allow these setbacks to slow you down. Every mistake you make provides an opportunity to learn. By acknowledging and embracing your mistakes, you can ensure that they do not happen again, smoothing the road to success. "Insanity is doing the same thing over and over again and expecting different results," said no less an authority.

**Do not be hesitant to put in some effort.**

Look no further than Bill Gates, the founder of Windows and one of the world's wealthiest businessmen, for proof of this piece of advice. The Microsoft founder has always emphasized that success comes from hard effort. Once admitted that he did not take a single day off when starting the company in his twenties. The more effort you put in, the more you'll receive out of it. "The price of success is hard work," as NFL legend Vince Lombardi once said. It does not get any more straightforward than that.

**Dare to be different.**

He knows a thing or two about fantasy life, having animated some of the most beloved fairy tales in the world. So when he says, "if you can think it, you can do it," pay attention. Aiming low may lessen the risk of making a mistake, but no great business man or woman has ever aimed low. If you are enthusiastic about a project and sincerely believe in it, you have every reason to believe you can reach your objectives. They may be closer than you believe!

**Pursue your interests.**

Finally, if you want to achieve great success in life, you must be passionate about doing. So, if you are an ambitious, high-flyer who wants to reach the very top, look closely at the things that interest and excite you. See if you can channel your enthusiasm into achieving your objectives.

### Do not Make Too Many Objectives

When we consider our goals, we frequently make a list and start writing down everything we want. Moreover, that is a fantastic way to begin started.

The difficulty is that we frequently wind up with an extensive list of tasks we want to accomplish, making it difficult to prioritize which ones are most important.

Instead, after you've completed your list, put some limits for yourself. For example, I only set five goals for myself each year. This means that I will be able to spend two months on each goal.

When you break down most goals, they all include changing or forming a habit. If you want to save £20,000 next year, for example, you'll need to alter your spending patterns. Spending less and saving more is a good strategy.

However, if you have a habit of going out shopping every weekend or spending an excessive amount of time on Amazon looking for the latest digital gadget, you will have to change your ways. Instead, you will need to become acquainted with your savings account. Then, instead of sending money to Amazon, make it a habit to send money to your savings account.

You have a lot higher chance of altering a habit if you give yourself two months to do so rather than changing many habits at once.

It is time to move on to your next aim once your habit has changed and become second nature.

## Look for connections

Look for links between your five goals once you have decided on them. When we define goals for ourselves, there is often a natural link between them.

An excellent example is losing weight and becoming in shape. There are two objectives here. Get in shape and lose weight. You may plan around the fact that the two naturally fit together.

## Establish Weekly Goals

The most challenging aspect of achieving goals, in my opinion, is keeping focused on them. We come face to face with the daily crises and challenges thrown at us after we have planned out what we want to achieve and become inspired and determined. It can be challenging to stay focused on our objectives when this happens.

To overcome this, set aside some time each week to develop one or two goals that will help you get closer to your goal.

For example, if your objective is to become in shape and lose weight, make a weekly target for how many times you will exercise and how much weight you want to lose. Set a goal to save £385 that week (or not, spend £385 that week) if your goal is to save £20,000 in the next year.

Breaking down your goals into smaller chunks like this helps you stay focused on the process. At the end of the week, the process will get you closer to your goals.

**Make a list of your objectives.**

You must first identify your objectives to achieve them. Allow yourself to be guided by your instincts rather than becoming overwhelmed by this process. Set a timer for three minutes and write down all of your objectives, regardless of how difficult they will be to achieve.

"Your head can be a dreadful workplace." That suggests your mind has a hard time remembering stuff. Make a list of your objectives.

Having your goals written down serves as a reminder. However, the following is the key to set down your objectives:

Keep it somewhere you will see it often.

It is pointless to write down your objectives on a piece of paper to have that piece of paper vanish behind a stack of other papers after a few days. Instead, if you keep a journal or diary, put down your objectives in it. If you use a digital notes app, make a list of your goals and pin them to the top of the list.

After this, consider what lifestyle changes or changes you will need to achieve your goals.

**Re-evaluate your objectives every week rather than daily.**

You quickly become numb to your goals if you read them every day. You get into the habit of just going through the motions of reading through a list, and the list eventually loses its power.

Instead, set aside some time on Sunday to ponder. Consider what you've completed this week and how you're progressing toward your goals. Examine where you are weak, where you've succumbed to temptation, and where you've fallen short. Then build a plan to ensure that the same thing does not happen the following week, and set one or two goals for yourself to achieve.

Your objectives will be more significant to you in this manner. You make weekly mini-goals for yourself that will help you get closer to your overall objectives.

**Have a compelling "Why.."**

A goal without reason for being is a flimsy goal. You must understand why you desire to achieve the goal.

Now, your "why" is personal, and explaining it to another person might be highly humiliating. The most important thing to remember is that the reason you want to achieve your objective must be YOUR reason, not someone else's.

While it is true that if you are a smoker and go to the doctor for a check-up, your doctor will tell you that you should quit smoking for your long-term health. It is not yours "why." If you enjoy smoking and are unconcerned about the long-term implications, then your "why" is weak.
The same is true when it comes to losing weight. You might be pretty content with your current weight. That is not your "why" if someone tells you that you should lose weight.

Your "why" should be personal, and it should have some emotional resonance with what you seek. An excellent personal "why" is "I want to reduce weight so I can look great at the beach." I have discovered that the more humiliating it is to tell someone your "why," the more influential the "why" becomes.

This guide might assist you in discovering your "why."

Goals are crucial in life because they provide you with a feeling of purpose, which gives you a reason to get up in the morning with vigour and passion.

Purpose helps you get through tough times and improves your general happiness and well-being.

If you follow these six golden guidelines for creating goals, you'll quickly find yourself accomplishing far more than you ever imagined. Best of luck!

## ...ON ACHIEVING YOUR OBJECTIVES

In life, everyone has a set of objectives. No matter who we are, we all aspire to do something. No matter how big or small. We do not always have the resources to see things through, in any case. We do not always dare to persevere through adversity and hardship to attain our objectives.

Quite often, we throw in the towel. We give up and call it a day. "Never again," "not another second," and "I am done!" are some of the phrases we use. It is not easy to go back after you have reached that tipping point. Nevertheless, it is not the case for everyone. Some of us are better at attaining our objectives than others. Some of us have learned to overcome failure.

How are we expected to see things through in a world where everything is available on-demand, a culture accustomed to having whatever we want when we want it? How are we meant to achieve our objectives when every fibre of our being begs us to surrender?
How can you reach your objectives?

Setting clearly defined goals and wanting them hard enough is not enough to achieve any life goal. It will help if you also employ the appropriate tactics to achieve them. You will not see things through if you do not go about it correctly, no matter what you want or how badly you think you want it.

Putting in place the necessary tactics to see things through is not a difficult or time-consuming endeavour. However, it necessitates consistent and persistent action. It is necessary to throw caution to the wind and endure massive suffering and hardship today to reap the benefits tomorrow.

You will see things through if you take the appropriate approach and have the right mindset. It is only a matter of time before it happens. Even if you get frustrated or face a few roadblocks along the way, you'll learn how to persevere. Instead of attempting to make things happen quickly, you'll discover how to manoeuvre around the obstacles by using the correct techniques to achieve in the long run.

|  | **GOALS** | **OBJECTIVES** |
|---|---|---|
| **Definition** | End result | Step by step towards the end result |
| **Timeframe** | Long-term | Medium to short-term |
| **Basis** | Ideas | Detailed facts |
| **Meaning** | A goal is a long-term vision of a desired outcome. | Objectives are each achievement (related to the goal) along the way |

## 1. Set SMARTER objectives.

The value of the SMARTER goal-setting process should be understood by anyone serious about reaching their objectives. Goals that are specific, measurable, achievable, relevant, time-bound, evaluated, and re-adjusted are smarter. It is a goal-setting method that has a high chance of success.

It will help if you are very explicit about your aim to set a SMARTER goal. Make sure it is measurable and achievable by describing it down to the last detail. For example, While ambitious long-term objectives are acceptable, SMARTER one-year goals should be slightly out of reach but still achievable.

Relevant means that the purpose must match your values and perspectives, as well as your inner identity. Simply put, time-bound means you have allocated a definite calendar date to its completion. Moreover, as you move toward your goal, you will need to rethink and change your strategy.

## 2. Make a strategy for moving forward.

One of the most crucial tactics for achieving any objective is planning. However, many of us fail to establish thorough and intricate strategies to help us achieve our goals. We have some vague idea in our heads that will only get us halfway there. But it will not help us achieve our objectives.

Anyone serious about achieving a goal must devise a comprehensive action plan and be willing to implement it daily. Every single day, without fail, to realize their dreams. Make a plan and obsess him, working out 24 hours a day, 7 days a week, until you reach your goals.

## 3. Get rid of undesirable behaviours.

Bad habits might prevent us from accomplishing our objectives. They hinder our advancement and obstruct our goals and dreams. Anyone who wants to do something great understands the importance of breaking bad habits that hold them back.

While breaking harmful habits is challenging, you can overcome them by identifying a more significant cause than the habit itself. It does not happen swiftly or without pain. It happens gradually and over time. However, by kicking your poor habits, you may easily pave the way to achieving your objectives.

## 4. Instil self-control.

Self-discipline enables us to put our goal attainment on autopilot. Anything is possible for someone disciplined. Any trivial chore can appear too onerous to a person who lacks self-discipline. Your habits are the surest path to becoming a self-disciplined person.

You may become self-disciplined by forming the proper habits in your life. Developing habits like waking up early, practising gratitude, eating well, exercising, and getting enough sleep can help us develop the self-discipline we need. Anything is feasible if you have the correct set of habits in your life.

## 5. Keep your distractions to a minimum.

Distractions obstruct our development, and the world is rife with them. The most prevalent source of distraction has been always-on pocket computers, which provide intimate access to the world's massive information archives. It is no surprise that staying productive during the day has become increasingly complex, given how mobile phones and social media have upended businesses and commerce, as well as how we engage with one another.

It will be best if you learn to block out the background noise. One technique for reaching your goals is to become aware of the distractions around you. Then attempt to eliminate them. Turn off the telephone, computer, and TV and immerse yourself in a world where you are exclusively focused on the task at hand.

Your workstation may resemble the perfect fantasy of a Pinterest addict. Nevertheless, if you do not eliminate additional sources of distraction, your minimalist workspace will be useless. Find a means to block family members, social media notifications, and personal phone calls and appointments (unless in an emergency). Even if no one is watching you, make a timetable for yourself and stick to it.

## 6. Use everyday goal-setting to your advantage.

Daily goals are an excellent method to stay focused and on track for your long-term objectives, which may be years away. When we try not to drown in our duties daily, it is easy to lose sight of those big ambitions. On the other hand, those daily targets provide indicators that are easier to keep to and focus on.

This technique necessitates setting goals every morning, without fail. What are your goals and objectives for today? Break down your monthly or 12-month goals into milestones.

It is easier to keep on track with whatever it is as long as it is measurable and broken down into what you need to accomplish that day.

## 7. Stay away from procrastination.

You may begin a task only to find yourself strolling over to the refrigerator, checking email, or Googling symptoms of an unknown ailment (we have all done it).

Procrastination is the silent assassin that prevents us from attaining our objectives. It stifles our advancement and forces us to withdraw into the safety and familiarity of our surroundings. Everyone understands that procrastination must be eliminated to do anything meaningful. Rather than waiting another day or minute, do what needs to be done right now.

Although procrastination may be inevitable, consider the 15-minute rule: The 15-minute rule is one approach for taking action and avoiding procrastination. Set a 15-minute timer on your phone and commit to accomplishing the one thing you have been putting off the most. It will just be for 15 minutes, no more. It is too tiny a commitment to fail. Once you do take action, you have just started building momentum. What are the chances? You can get into a groove and not want to quit when the timer goes off. After that, you might as well keep going.

## 8. Keep track of your time.

Becoming efficient in time management is one approach to achieving anything in life. Those who are the best at managing their time are the ones who can achieve lofty objectives. To accomplish this, you must establish an effective method for managing the limited time you have rather than wasting it.

Use the quadrant time management strategy to divide your time into four distinct quadrants. Concentrate as much of your efforts as possible on Quadrant 2 while avoiding Quadrant 4 as much as possible. Examine how much time you spend in each of these quadrants during the day.

|  | Urgent | Not Urgent |
|---|---|---|
| Important | **Quadrant 1**<br><br>Crisis<br>Pressing problems<br>Deadlines | **Quadrant 2**<br><br>Personal growth<br>Long-term planning<br>Relationship building |
| Not Important | **Quadrant 3**<br><br>Interruptions<br>Popular activities<br>Some meetings/calls | **Quadrant 4**<br><br>Time wasters<br>Escape activities<br>Trivia |

## 9. Make a bee-line towards the frog.

As Mark Twain famously put it, "It is preferable to eat a frog first thing in the morning if it is your job. It is also advisable to eat the largest frog first if you have to consume two frogs." He was talking to the big-ticket tasks on your to-do list, the ones that would help you achieve your long-term objectives the most.

You are chasing the frog in this method by attacking your MITs first thing in the morning. Make sure you tackle those huge Quadrant 1 jobs first thing in the morning to get them out of the way. While you may not notice immediate effects from your activities, they add up in the long run. Do it first thing in the morning, when you are well-rested.

## 10. Put the Pareto Principle in action.

The Pareto Principle, commonly known as the 80/20 Rule, argues that 20% of the effort yields 80% of the results. In sales, this also means that 20% of the clients account for 80% of the sales. However, it further shows that among the 20% that provide 80% of the results, 20% of that subset creates 80% of the results.

What is the point? Concentrate your efforts on scaling up the limited number of activities that are yielding the most significant effects. To implement this method, you must first determine which initiatives are yielding the most results. Nevertheless, all you have to do now is scale up your efforts. You have done that.

## 11. Failure is a good thing.

While some may not consider failure a plan for success, it is one of the safest strategies to achieve the goals in any effort. Furthermore, some of the most well-known persons on the planet have failed numerous times. They differ from the rest of us in that they did not surrender.

When failure knocks on your door, learn to greet it with open arms. It is okay. It is obvious. Take what you've learned. After that, you can get on with your life. Use your setbacks as opportunities to learn and try again. "Failure is merely an opportunity to start over, this time more sensibly," Henry Ford once stated.

## 12. Find ways to be inspired every day.

While we all desire to do something significant in our lives, we frequently become disheartened despite our best efforts to persevere and see things through. The damaging thinking gears start churning. The what-if the doomsday scenarios start playing out in our heads as soon as this happens.

Fear emerges from the darkness, ready to suffocate us and prevent us from reaching our objectives. You must seek daily doses of inspiration to combat this. Make contact with those who have already achieved the results you want. Listen to what they have to say and try to put yourself in their shoes. How did they deal with failure after failure? How did they recover and reach their objectives?

## 13. Look for a role model.

At the very least, navigating the choppy waters of commerce and industry can be disastrous. We do not always know which way to sail when we are out on the water. Our ship can fill up with water and sink when we do not know what to do next to stay afloat. Finding a mentor can assist you in surviving and achieving your goals.

Mentors serve to illuminate a route to achievement by shining a light on it. They assist us in achieving our objectives, like a beacon in the night that shines brilliantly through the foggy fog. To ensure survival and ultimate success, they know which direction to travel in and often avoid treacherous waters.

## 14. Maintain a record of your achievements.

You must track your progress if you are serious about achieving something. You can analyse and alter your efforts to meet your objectives if you track your progress. If you do not keep track, you have no idea where you are, how far you've come, or how much longer you have to go.

Construct a tracking system. You can track your goals if they are measurable. Every day, keep track of them. You must track your progress to confirm that what you are doing is working, much like a plane would chart and track its path from moment to moment. You are losing time if you do not keep rigorous track of your objectives.

## 15. Be open to feedback.

People are quick to judge others, especially when they see them succeed. They try to bring you down. When you do succeed, they are there to remind you that you should not have attempted that lofty objective in the first place.

That criticism should be welcomed. Do not flee. Pay attention to what they have to say. Use it to motivate you to reach your objectives rather than hold you back. Each of us makes mistakes. We have more chances to succeed the more times we fail. It should not matter what other people think if you desire something. Rather than holding you back, use it to propel and push you forward.

## 16. Maintain a tidy working environment.

Clutter is proven to distract you, not just physically. Consider it a mental, as well as a physical, disaster. Extra items on your desk compete for your attention, forcing your brain to continuously reconcile their appearance with those that are genuinely relevant to your task. Consider some of the things that hang around for a long time that may leave you now. Ask yourself an essential inquiry about any stuff you may feel emotionally attracted to: Is this thing inspiring me to attain my goals, or is it serving another purpose?

## 17. Get out of bed as soon as possible.

It might be challenging to stay concentrated during the day, no matter how hard you try to isolate yourself from daily distractions like children, errands, or even the news. Getting up early has helped several successful entrepreneurs find time to focus on their goals. Sure, our bodies are conditioned to wake up simultaneously every day. It will take some time to adjust. You will not be able to add three hours to your morning routine in a single day. Being an early riser needs planning, patience, and mental clarity.

## 18. Make the most of your free time on the weekends.

While it is vital to relax and rejuvenate during the weekend, it is also a good idea to plan for your week, including how you'll achieve your objective. Do not let the alarm clock sound fill you with the dread of tedious activities when you wake up on Monday morning. Set aside some time on Sunday night to plan your clothing for the next day or week, schedule meals, and organize your to-do list. You will sleep better, feel less stressed, and have more time to devote to the career you love.

## 19. Enlist the assistance of others.

You would be crazy to believe that you can achieve success on your own, no matter how motivated you are. Even if someone else is not directly assisting you, it is beneficial to identify a few people you can look up to who can motivate you to persevere or hold you accountable.

For example, a mentor might provide valuable guidance not to learn basic things the hard way. You might benefit from having a cheerleader or sidekick to keep you motivated and accountable. Locate specific individuals who can assist you in bridging the gap between where you are and where you want to go.

Do not do it alone. There is only so far a project can go before it necessitates a change of perspective. This may be anything. Perhaps you're training for a half marathon and cannot seem to get your PB under the desirable 2-hour mark no matter how hard you try. At this stage it might be a good idea to seek advice from a friend.

## 20. Take on the job.

Consider whom you want to be. What will your new-and-improved self-behave like? What will you think, say, and do? You will probably want to present yourself as a humble but confident individual. Instead of slouching, sit up straight. Instead of looking away or letting your thoughts roam, look into their eyes and hear what they have to say. Make a conscious effort to choose your words. Success is more likely to follow if you can learn from others, make a good impression, and discipline yourself to show the world your real ambitions.

## 21. Check in on your progress regularly.

It is not enough to adopt new behaviours and abandon old ones. To stay on track, you must schedule a time to review yourself regularly. Schedule quarterly review sessions if you have met smaller goals that will lead you to a larger goal or if you have set a deadline (say a year). Reflect on what you've been doing. Whether it is working or how you may revise your plan during these check-ins with yourself. Allow your accomplishments to motivate you to keep going.

## 22. Use incentives to keep oneself motivated.

You will have an added incentive to persevere if you create prizes for yourself once you've completed mini-milestones in addition to the larger objective. Reaching a particular number of followers on social media, getting up at 4 a.m. for the first time in a week, or saving an extra £1,000, £5,000, or £10,000 are all examples of milestones. You may spoil yourself with a favourite dish, a spa treatment, new recreational equipment, or simply a relaxing day off. Whatever the situation, make sure your incentive system is appealing enough to inspire you to work hard while remaining modest enough to be long-term sustainable.

# CONCLUSION

## THE SINGLE MOST IMPORTANT THING YOU REQUIRE TO REALIZE YOUR GOALS

When focused attention, goal-setting, and purposeful activity all fall into place, a quality life emerges. Whether you achieve your ambition of becoming or not is primarily determined by your actions.

The treatment for procrastination's maladies is a heavy dose of action, at least until the day comes when your dreams and their realizations are the same. Dream more giant dreams and take more action when that day arrives.

A good strategy will nearly always get you in the door, but action will cement the deal. So you are looking for a guarantee? Well, here it is: Failure and mediocrity are the only guarantees without deliberate action!

Before it waltzes off into the arms of neglect, do not tiptoe toward your goal. Move confidently. Dreams come true thanks to one basic form of transportation: deliberate action.

It is like addiction to weapons of mass destruction if you keep destructive behaviours like procrastination and poor follow-through.

Procrastination is fatally uncool. Unfortunately, most people never realize their full potential. There is never an opening night, never a debut.

The majority of potential is hidden deep within each person, waiting to be released. It remains hidden because people are fearful. The mechanics of reaching a goal make it simple for individuals to understand the importance of taking action.

We are always disorganized and confused when we operate without forethought. You are always busy, yet you do not get anything done. The most you can hope for is minimal progress without a deeper understanding and use of planning.

You must be entirely sure that this is what you are supposed to be doing with your life because your commitment to this one area is so deep. You may justifiably rule out all other options.

We find the potential for greatness when we focus all of our attention and have tunnel vision for something we both enjoy and are naturally skilled at. You cannot be great at something if you do not love it and are not naturally skilled. Sure, luck plays a role. But you only have one opportunity at living your best life if you take it.

People will tell you otherwise, but following your passion, above all a talent, is the best thing you will ever do. You are giving yourself the best chance to be great in life and create the kind of life that is uniquely and genuinely yours by taking that path. Never forget that those opposed to your desire or trying to impose reality on your dream parade are frequently envious of you for having one in the first place.

You will almost certainly meet the most opposition and pushback from individuals in your circle, such as family and old friends. It is one of the most challenging things to realize. It does not matter how confident you are in your abilities and the future. You are attempting to build for yourself.
That is okay. It is not because of them. They are only trying to keep an eye out for you. However, it will be best if you remember that everybody who offers an opinion on what you're doing is doing so through their biased lens. So when people try to tell you what you "should be doing," they are speaking from a skewed perspective based on their own

beliefs. Boundaries are ingrained in them by their parents, who were instilled in them by their parents.

When you face obstacles, you must maintain your self-confidence and vision for the future. When we face opposition from our peers, friends, and family, it is all too easy to feel overwhelmed by self-doubt and melancholy because our self-belief conviction might get thrown off track.

I have discovered four techniques for safeguarding my dream and maintaining my conviction and self-belief in its direction:

Remove people in your life who are not supportive of your goals. This is a brutal tactic. Nevertheless, do it if your dream is so important to you. You are being your most authentic self by pursuing it. Why surround yourself with people who do not support you in your quest to be your best self? The truth is that they either do not understand, do not see, or do not think what they believe is achievable.

Create a more extensive network of people on the same path as you and help you achieve your goals. Finding a group of friends who work in the same field as you and whom you believe to be more successful than you is the best method to do this. You will be able to "level up" and expect more of yourself due to this. In an ideal world, you'd locate a core group of people with whom you can exchange ideas, provide feedback, and all assist each other flourish and reach your objectives.

This is the most significant. It is all about gaining traction. When you keep your momentum, you keep your self-confidence. How can you keep the momentum going? Concerning work. When you stop working, your anxiety rises. Your self-doubt grows, and you become stuck in a rut. However, when you work hard and put in the necessary time and effort to master your skill, inspiration strikes, and you begin to feel great about yourself and confident about your path. The devil (doubt) is silenced at work, and angels are invoked (inspiration). Starting small and temporarily scaling down your ambitions are the key to regaining momentum after losing it. When I am stuck in a rut with my writing, my goal is to write one awful page. That is all. From there, I gradually add more and more each day until rolling. Your significant goals are once again attainable.

Now, self-confidence is crucial. However, what destroys self-confidence is when people set unrealistic goals for themselves. The majority of individuals desire it right now. They are impatient. They want it to prove sceptics wrong as soon as possible. They cannot stay strong and play the long game without it. Because it is such a long journey, the most challenging aspect of pursuing artistic aspirations is overcoming resistance. It is not like running a business where you can make money right away. It takes years, if not decades, to hone your profession and become proficient enough. Success manifests itself in a form that others can recognize or identify with.

For example, one of my ambitions is to write for some of Hollywood's most popular television shows and win an Emmy for writing. Sure, that is a lofty objective. Nevertheless, it becomes much more achievable when you pair it with patience and a realistic schedule. It is about trusting that those external "benchmarks of success" will start to arrive at you when you are ready. All is possible when you have given your art enough time to marinate and have grown in love with the process of what you are doing rather than the goal of "doing it,"

It will help if you allow yourself to be wrong and have strong self-belief and patience to play the long game toward the objective. They are terrified and anxious when they see how vast the gap is between their current level of skill and aptitude. Where their ambitions and dreams lay, many people never follow what they have always dreamed of doing or give up so quickly. To put it another way, most people are incapable of enduring the early years of sucking. They want to do the right thing right away and for it to pay off right away.

As a result, they walk away from it with their tails between their legs, pursuing a less challenging road that will allow them to benefit more rapidly. A road that does not force them to face the kind of hard effort and perseverance that is required to succeed.

This is where you can tell the difference between folks who genuinely desire it and others who glamorize the concept of achieving it. For example, consider one actor who wants to perform desperately. The musician wants to be a famous rock star but does not want to play their music for free to drunks in a pub for years. Alternatively, those who want to be entrepreneurs want to be "wealthy" and "Ballin" rather than tackle real-world problems.

The only way to bridge the gap between your talent and expertise and your noble goals and dreams is to put a great deal of effort into it. A passion for the job. A genuine, unwavering commitment to the process. We are born with talent. On the other hand, our expertise is something we create via a religious devotion to the process. Moreover, after enough time has passed for our talent and expertise to marinate, the shores of our ambitions begin to break through the fog.

It does not matter what you hold onto. Above all, you must believe in the viability of the vision you have in your head.

Even if others roll their eyes and scoff at it, you must see it, smell it, and taste it with every fibre in your body.

It is up to you to safeguard your dream, which you do by nurturing your self-belief and surrounding yourself with people who inspire you. You achieve this by gaining momentum by consistently putting in the effort. You achieve this by committing to the long game. You do so by trusting the process and realizing that you will achieve success if you focus on getting better and enjoying the process rather than on being successful. You do this by having the bravery to fail and be judged and condemned by others. You do so by being so passionate about what you're doing that you're willing to do it for free for years on end. You can do this by treating yourself with kindness and speaking to yourself as if you're someone you admire and respect. All while committing to being the person you need to be.

# Disclaimer

This book contains opinions and ideas of the author and is meant to teach the reader informative and helpful knowledge while due care should be taken by the user when applying the information provided. The instructions and strategies are possibly not right for every reader and there is no guarantee that they work for everyone. Using this book and implementing the information contained is explicitly your own responsibility and risk. This work with all its contents, does not guarantee correctness, perfection or completion of the information provided. Misinformation or misprint cannot be completely eliminated.

What You Think Becomes Your Reality

***Thanks for reading!***
***Please add a review on Amazon and***
***let me know what you thought!***

Amazon reviews are extremely helpful for authors, thank you for taking the time to support me and my work.

**Reginaldo Gattward**

Printed in Great Britain
by Amazon